The Girl at the Door

The Girl at the Door

A LIFE DURING
THE GOLDEN AGE OF HOLLYWOOD
& WHAT HAPPENED AFTERWARD

BY
DIANE DU BOIS

Girl at the Door Publications
© 2019 by Diane Du Bois

Dedication

I am especially grateful to my brother George. I could not have written this book without his help and photographic memory. George Du Bois ran for congress in Hawaii, but he didn't win. He had a brilliant mind and would have been perfect for the job. After all, it's one's thoughts that count.

To the rest of my family, Kevin and Susanne McConnell and their four sons, Patrick, Oliver, Nicholas and Sean; who is serving his country in the Navy; and to Breffni and his wife Maribelle, who gave me loving support.

Acknowledgments

Kevin, my eldest son, who when I decided to write a comedy about my weird tenants, told me to include them in a story about my life.

Susanne, his wife, who made my life comfortable and beautiful.

Nicole Zugsmith, my step-granddaughter, who worked on my "fear factor," the computer, and organized my work.

Patrick, my youngest grandson, who while I hand wrote my script, typed it all.

And finally to Jessie Buchanan, who designed my cover and with her knowledge and artistry, helped me put my book together, for which I am eternally grateful.

TABLE OF CONTENTS

FOREWORD

The Girl At The Door chronicles my life's stories from a Europe reeling from the second of two world wars as a refugee family adjusts to American Culture. I was brought into the Hollywood of celluloid dreams at the age of six because I spoke French. I met many famous people on a simple non-theatrical level...Cary Grant, Marlon Brando, etc.

My first husband was an Irish actor. My second a Hungarian freedom fighter. I was exposed to many different aspects of life; taking care of six children (two of my own!), sexual assault, dementia, the tyranny of tenants, corruption, bankruptcy, the heartbreak of betrayal, and finally...the seduction of the supernatural. This book is based on my understanding of these events. I wrote about the people I knew best - from the filmmaking Hollywood I knew in the 1940's as a child actress. Also, the interesting backgrounds which made these people decide to move to America. As I look back, it's just the stories of life. I named most of the chapters with movie titles I thought appropriate.

Chapter 1

Topolino

While *IL Duce* (Benito Mussolini) was famously making the trains run on time in Italy, two other events were taking place. Fiat, the automaker of Torino, was not only contributing to the fascist war effort but also designing and fabricating an adorable modest little coupe that thousands of Italians and other Europeans gratefully called Topolino. The name was taken from a lovable cartoon mouse featured in the daily paper, and in cinemas, filled with the shrieks and laughter of black-shirted children watching the antics of a mouse and his friends, Walt Disney's Mickey Mouse, known as Topolino in Rome, Napoli, and Firenze.

With its smiling front grill, two big headlights and open doors looking like ears, the small coupe warmed its way into the heart of Grandmother Mettewie (Meme, pronounced may may). Little did she think it would become transportation for two adults, three children, baggage, containers of fuel, and a mattress on its roof; however, Meme was not a conventional rocking chair Granny, but a lady adventurer with talent and courage as one of the first women who drove a car in 1900 when most men navigating by horse and carriage and looked at the motorized ones dismissing them as noisy unreliable passing fads. Meme turned out to belong to the future and was never without a car well into her old age (1883-1976).

When General Juderian's Wehrmacht Panzers crossed the Belgian border in the spring of 1940 in a repeat performance of 1914, it was decided by three adults - Meme, Maman, and Papa - that Topolino would transport the two ladies and three children to Spain by way of France to rejoin Papa who had gone off to California the previous year. Papa had sensed war and German occupation coming but one thing is known for sure - he detested the North Sea Belgian climate and it was a long held dream to live and work in California. He was an established philatelist with his own stamp shop on a major Brussels commercial thoroughfare, the Boulevard Adolplhe Max. The American immigration law at that time was based on a quota system that favored people from northwest European countries (the Belgian quotas were never filled), and if you had the means of support and had no communicative disease, you qualified for entry into the USA. The family qualified on all counts.

Next door to Papa's shop was an exotic tropical fruit shop, displaying on silk and velvet cloths fruits almost never seen in those days in Brussels - pineapples, coconuts, peaches, papayas. And it was interestingly called - in large, capital gold letters across the display window - CALIFORNIA. In the display background one could see travel posters featuring California tourist destinations - Yosemite, San Francisco, Hollywood, Sequoia, and others. For most it seemed pure fantasy, for Papa it seemed perfect except for the finances.

By a happy coincidence an opportunity presented itself by the 1936 Olympic Games. While Maman (mother) was expecting me four years after my older brother Youri was born, Papa was out of town, attending the Berlin games, to purchase as many copies of the commemorative Olympic stamps issued by the Third Reich as his limited funds would allow. Philately (stamp collecting) had always been popular among German customers who were regular visitors to his Brussels shop. It even improved his knowledge of the language. The German postal authorities promoted Philately by issuing interesting semi-postal stamps - those are the ones where a part of the postage fee collected was distributed to organizations like the Red Cross or Winter Help. Papa's foresight not only financed the move to California, but served him for many years in California during the war, especially when souvenir sheets from an enemy country were very much in demand and fetched a nice profit.

The last child was born in 1937 named Jean Jacques, a blue-eyed blonde much resembling his father. Two years later Papa sailed to America on the glamorous new French liner Normandy, and he had his first taste of Hollywood meeting Shirley Temple, the famous child star, as a fellow passenger. His previous experience with the cinema was taking Youri to Laurel and Hardy comedies in dark and dank, odorous and smoky theaters, with French subtitles of course, and no popcorn in those days. When Papa arrived in New York, he was the guest of the biggest stamp wholesaler Julius Stolow, whom he met previously at a philatelic convention in Hamburg. He crossed the country in a five day voyage in the 20th Century Limited to Los Angeles, and wrote a letter to Maman about how he was looking forward to the family's arrival and how he missed us, but his real enthusiasm was how impressive the new country was and how he immediately saw it as a country of opportunity.

Although he was impressed by New York, he had no intention of staying there to suffer a continuation of northern European weather. Maman had named her eldest Youri (Russian for George, which is what he went by once we moved to America). Part of the reason was that she was hostile to the Catholic church and religion in general. She belonged to that generation of Europeans who believed that science and rational thinking had replaced religion, and she was not going to give her son a name reflecting the holy faith such as her own Marie Jose. She named me Diane, one of the fashionable first names of the time and conscientiously non-Christian. World War II had yet to demonstrate the fallacy of faith in science and so-called reason.

Maman was reluctant to leave her familiar and comfortable upper class environment where she had been presented at court - after all she was the granddaughter of the respected Burgomeister of Molenbeek St. Jean, Louis Mettwie, who been reelected many times to hold the office for 56 years. Each borough of Brussels had its own Burgomeister and he was the most famous. Years later, Boulevard Louis Mettwie was named in his honor. Before Paris built its famous metro, Louis Mettwie attempted to have one developed in Brussels, but he was not successful. With its failure, Louis Mettwie made one of his famous speeches, starting with "Mes dames et messieurs, it is with tears in my eyes that I report," etc., etc. He was a consummate politician, he was beloved. He was also a 33rd degree Mason. Many dinner parties were held with politicians from all over the world attending, and Maman was allowed to attend because of her quick mind and good looks. She was often compared to Queen Ingrid of Sweden in appearance.

Maman used to tell her own family of the unpleasant side of the Belgian spirit. Often, when the maids were serving dinner, the odor of their perspiration was so strong, the grandparents would complain.

Maman would comment, "But you ration their soap, what do you expect?"

And while picking the strawberries in the garden (Meme's second husband was a famous horticulturist), the maids were forced to whistle all the while to prevent them from eating the precious berries.

Maman was voted Queen of the May, which mirrored an attitude she carried throughout her lifetime.

Maman's father, the Comte Armand du Bois d'Arencourt, passed away at the age of 33. He was a champion runner, ran his race, gulped down a glass of cold water and died.

All was being readied for our tearful departure and goodbyes, never to meet again. The three of us - 8, 4 and 3 years old - all crowded into the Topolino and the five of us made our way to the road to Paris, France.

In 1940, the road to Paris consisted of two lanes, not always smooth and uniform and certainly not accustomed to the heavy traffic they were about to experience. The average Belgian did not possess a car then and the road began to fill with horse-drawn carts, filled with household possessions, shepherds with flocks of sheep, farmers with livestock from cows to pigs to geese, ducks and chickens, old trucks overflowing with women often accompanied by men walking along the side of the vehicles, cigarettes hanging from their mouths, wearing greasy hats and caps, sometimes with leashed Shepherd dogs, and grunting to show authority what little control they possessed.

The crude sounds of Flemish, mixed with the softer ones of French, one had the impression that everyone was going out of his or her way to misunderstand each other and be as uncooperative as each could to emphasize the class, education and income level as though in their shared misery, any of these things would make any difference. However, one may assume that illusions of the mind are often stronger than any collective reality. Anyone with a horn abused it by beeping loudly and frequently with no positive results other than scaring horses and receiving insulting shouts and vulgar signs. As if all this panicky chaos was not bad enough, from the opposite direction came British tanks. Scouts went ahead of their column and attempted to give direction to civilians to make way, adding to the surrealism of the situation. It led to one additional cast of characters, the men from the Luftwaffe who felt the necessity to strafe the whole lot by sending down low flying Messerschmitts combined with Stuka bombers to create a fiery havoc by dropping incendiary bombs. The Topolino bailed out into a ditch along Road 31.

Maman was asking, "What have I done?"

At 57, Meme might have thought that this was worse than the war of 1914.

Taking side roads to Paris, finding food, shelter, and fuel for the Topolino are a vague memory, but Meme was resourceful. Five weeks after the departure from Brussels, the Topolino arrived at the Spanish border. The queue of refugees was somewhat quieter and this particular group consisted mainly of people who no longer felt safe in France under the German occupation. The combined forces – Gendarmes, French soldiers, Wehrmacht - examined the obligatory documents, turning back many of the disappointed families. Meme and Maman seemed to possess the correct papers, and the Topolino was waved on minus the contraband pistol.

The aftermath of the civil war in Spain left a lot of scars, both physical and emotional. There was a shortage and milk, bread, and coins but since Meme and Maman had resources the children often had cake, hot chocolate and ice cream, as would have suggested Marie Antoinette under the circumstances. Youri played the role of the liaison between the outside world and the family because of his linguistic ability and his eagerness to be the man of the family.

The family was housed in a roomy and airy apartment, ironically facing the German consulate, its entire facade covered by a gigantic swastika-crested red banner. For some reason Maman held some negative opinions of Spaniards. Could it be that she considered them too macho? That would be in direct contradiction with the high esteem she held for Italians. Maman was a woman's libber of sorts.

The family was allowed to remain in Spain when very few people were in that position, and the subsequent permission to depart for America, perhaps it was the combination of inside favoritism combined with dollars from Meme, who was far from destitute. Years later Papa was to accuse Meme of helping herself to Maman's inheritance, which turned out to be true.

On a gray morning Meme left us to sail for the Belgian Congo in Africa, a place of opportunity for dislocated Belgians. Destiny was not quite finished with her. She opened a hotel and was prosperous until the Mau-Mau rebellion of 1954.

One morning, two of her long-time employees came into the kitchen and as she was giving instructions for the day. They looked at her grinning and said, "Not today Mama. Today we have to keel you" and with that took out their long knives.

Meme always carried a concealed gun and with undeniable courage shot them both dead. In all the confusion she was able to flee the Country. Isn't it ironic how Meme was driven from Belgium by White Supremacists and later driven from the Congo by Black Supremacists?

Meanwhile, the rest of the family was off by Air Madrid. In 1940 commercial flights in Spain were recently established, and what today would be a short hop seemed like an eternity. Our first flight was on-board the workhouse of Lufthansa for passengers and the Luftwaffe for soldiers, the reliable but homely Junkers 52 - three engines, wicker seats and extremely noisy. The aircraft's interior looked like a Quonset hut with aluminum siding.

The second part of the journey was changing planes and arriving in Lisbon. During the war now raging in Europe, it enjoyed a reputation as a city full of great night life, nervous refugees negotiating, bribing officials, and waiting for papers and tickets that would allow them to take voyages to the Americas. Agents represented both sides simultaneously as Portugal was neutral.

It was in Lisbon that the family ran into the infamous Tant Rina, Papa's sister, who had married a Russian nobleman. One has to understand in Russia in that era, everyone seemed to have a title. Papa said in his neighborhood he was the only one without one. Papa and his sister at a very young age fled the Bolshevik revolution of 1917. Because of their status in society, which guaranteed their elimination, Papa and Rina, who had learned French in school, found their way to Paris, a favorite location of Russian émigrés that had escaped the horrors of Soviet Communism with the help of Nansen passports, issued to stateless people by the League of Nations.

Papa, who was an apprentice to a stamp dealer (in order to eat), excelled because of his knowledge of history and geography. He became a philatelist, (a fancy word for stamp dealer) and Rina because of her unusual beauty ended up in Berlin at UFA GmbH studios (a German film and television production company that unites all production activities of Bertelsmann in Germany).

She was no longer Krassowski but Rina Marsa, UFA was the biggest studio in the silent days. Joseph Goebbels, who became propaganda minster under Hitler, fired everyone who did not speak German like a native, typical of politician's hypocritical double standard. He had a Czech mistress. He also attended many theatrical social functions, some attended by the Vatican Papal Nuncio to Germany, the future Pope Pius XII. Rina Marsa was a guest as well. Talkies had come and that was the end of her career. She had made at least thirteen pictures by then. Rina had had a very close relationship with Marlene Dietrich (who was a German actress and singer who held both German and American citizenship, her long career spanned from 1910 to the 1980s, maintained popularity by continually reinventing herself). Rina often wore slacks, being very influenced by Dietrich, but she had her own elegance. Maman told me that Rina was one of the most beautiful women that she had ever met, with her violet eyes, dark hair, and classic features, often wearing a small bunch of violet to accentuate her eyes. Despite her good looks, it didn't seem to make her happy. It did open doors, but if one is not emotionally equipped, sometimes it's a hindrance.

Unfortunately she had a rather vicious tongue, but she was always extremely generous. Rina lived on fashionable Ave Foche in Paris, not very far from the Duke and Duchess of Windsor. In 1937 during the World Exposition, Maman and Youri were guests in her lavish apartment filled with blue tinged mirrors and wall-to-wall white carpeting, which was the rage at that time. The rumors of Rina and the Windsors were circulating and talked about at parties that Maman attended. Papa was very old school and remained frozen-faced when the subject came up about his sister.

Three years later, Meme and family in the Topolino passed by Rina's apartment in Paris and encouraged her to go to Spain, which she did, another misfortune for Rina, Mussolini turned down the Italian ambassador's request to wed Rina. The Mussolini fascist government was the very essence of nationalism, so it was no surprise that it turned its ambassador down in his request to wed a foreigner, especially one who was, as the expression of the era was, "a kept woman."

Later when my dear Aunt "Tante Rina" came to stay with us for a prolonged visit in the United States, she was greeted warmly as her generosity, selling many gifts of fine jewelry, some probably from the Windsors, helped finance our trip. Tante Rina explained to Youri, Jean Jacque, and me that if we misbehaved, she had many belts of different colors that inflicted different levels of pain depending on the color. I was puzzled and told my Mother who explained to me at a later date. At that time, "dominatrix" (a dominating woman, especially one who takes the sadistic role in sadomasochistic sexual activities) was not part of my vocabulary.

The day of embarkation finally arrived as the family boarded the American freighter/passenger ship USS Exeter. Maman was to meet a man also bound for Hollywood, California, one Michael Curtiz, destined to become a celebrated film director (he was a Hungarian-born American film director, recognized as one of the most prolific directors in history).

One of our first introductions to Yankee cuisine was lime Jell-O on a bed of lettuce with a dash of mayonnaise. As the green gelatin shook and shimmied with the swaying of the ship, Maman assumed it was a living jellyfish and told us kids to avoid it. The next shock was how wasteful the culinary crew was when they pitched large amounts of leftovers out of the porthole windows.

The most exciting moment was during the life saving drill on deck. They had a touch of reality when a German U-Boat (the "U" means "undersea boat") surfaced at that exact moment - sighs of relief when the submarine commander presented the liner with a smart salute, two other officers in the tower waving in friendly greeting, swastika banner briskly waving in the breeze; America was still neutral, with Pearl Harbor a year away (the attack on Pearl Harbor was a surprise military strike by the Imperial Japanese Navy Air Service against the United States naval base at Pearl Harbor, Hawaii Territory, on the morning of December 7, 1941.)

As the USS Exeter entered the port of New York, the Statue of Liberty greeting passengers, with her traditional welcome and promise of better things to come.

We were met at the port by Julius Stolow, the most prominent philatelic wholesaler in the United States. The family climbed in to what seemed to be a bus. It was actually a 1941 Oldsmobile four-door convertible, top up. Soon we were on the slick road to Pelham, an upper crust suburb. The car pulled up to one of those driveways leaving my family's first impression of the expansive atmosphere in America, making Europe seem cramped by contrast. Two days later we were delivered to Grand Central Station on the 20th Century Limited bound for Los Angeles, California. The train took seven days. When we arrived at Union Station in Los Angeles, we immediately noticed the weather had become so mild. Maman and Papa reunited after an absence of almost two years. Finally, we had arrived.

Great Grandfather Louis Mettewie Burgomeister of Molenbeek Belgium

Louis Mettewie and his wife

Mother and younger Jean Jacques (JJ)

Mother and older brother Youri (George)

*My father's sister **Rina Marsa.***
(Headshot Ufa pictures, Berlin)

Autographed promotional photo
of my aunt. (Ufa pictures, Berlin)

My aunt and my father after escaping Russia

My mother and father

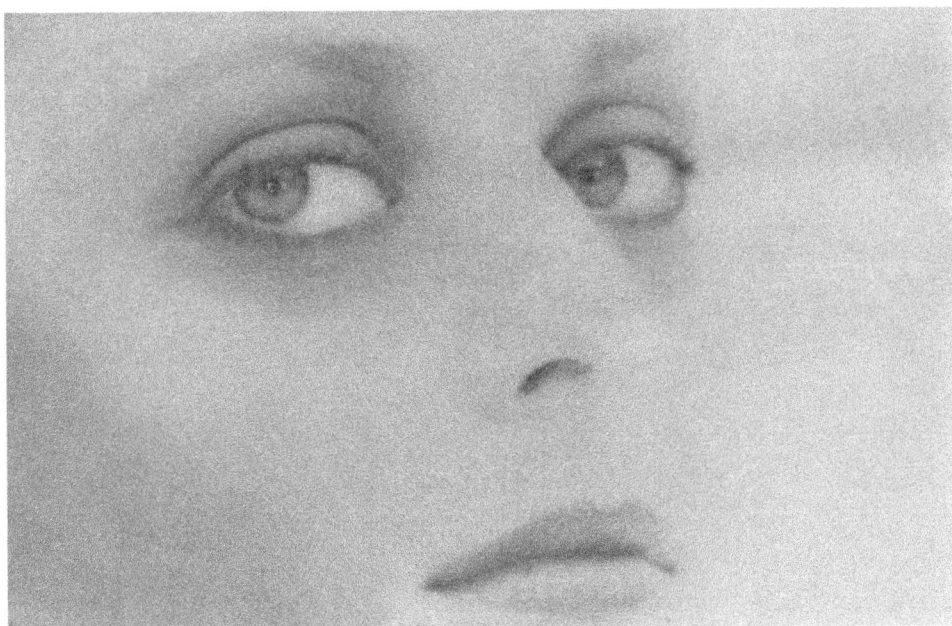

My aunt Rina Marsa, Ufa pictures, Berlin

Early publicity shot of Diane DuBois

Chapter 2

Hollywood

The Film Industry of Hollywood had declared war against Nazi Germany before the United States officially did. The British actors and actresses in particular were beating the drums for Americans to participate one way or another in saving England. British war relief drives in Hollywood, Edward R. Murrow reporting from a London rooftop (Mr. Murrow was an American broadcast journalist and war correspondent. He first gained prominence during World War II with a series of live radio broadcasts from Europe for the news division of the Columbia radio broadcasts from Europe). Dodging the bombs of the Luftwaffe (this was the aerial warfare branch of the combined German Wehrmacht military forces during World War II). Charlie Chaplin in *The Great Dictator,* Jack Benny portraying the brave Poles fighting the Gestapo in the memorable *To Be or Not to Be,* (was an American entertainer of the 20th century, portrayed a comedian, on vaudevillian, on radio, television and film actor, and violinist. Benny portrayed his character as a miser, playing his violin badly), and countless other anti-

Nazi comedies and tragedies were designed to soften the most isolationist citizens to sympathize and lend a hand to defeat Hitler.

The president initiated the lifesaving "Lend Lease Act" at Churchill's pleading, (Sir Winston Leonard Spencer-Churchill was a British politician, army officer, and writer, who was Prime Minister of the United Kingdom from 1940 to 1945 and again from 1951 to 1955)

A Yank in the Royal Air Force was another strong indicator. That was the prevailing atmosphere in movie land Hollywood, where motion pictures were actually being shot in the studios of Paramount, Universal, Columbia, United Artists, and Warner Brothers.

The first house on Meadow Brook Avenue makes one think of a babbling brook with weeping willows; however, Meadow Brook Avenue was in a middle class suburban neighborhood of Los Angeles. Not knowing locations or real-estate values, Papa plunked down his first American dollars for a standard duplex. He liked the idea of having tenants making the payments on the property. It was a culture shock that the tenants who paid Papa their rent drove an expensive car while he rode the bus to work, to his stamp shop on Hollywood Boulevard. Papa reasoned it was a matter of priorities.

Joseph was a hefty blue-collar type, somewhat leery of foreigners, with a frail wife Clara, who had a Brooklyn accent. When Maman was introduced to them, Joe did not get up, sitting on the couch with bare feet up on the coffee table.

When he did finally get up, he slapped Maman on the back and said "Hi, Josie."

In the garden one day, Joe and Maman were talking and Maman said, "I'm going in to take a douche," the French word for shower.

Joe's eyes bulged as he replied, "You French girls are certainly fast." Joseph was a bottomless pit of kindness and helpfulness.

On June 22nd, 1941, Papa announced that the Germans had invaded Russia. It was a bad decision to create a two-front war. History tells that when Napoleon did the same thing in 1812. Papa pinned a colored map on his wall for his customers who had a variety of opinions about the war. A while later the prompt Japanese gardener failed to show up. Two weeks later, a furtive elderly man wearing a helmet came to the door, introducing himself as the block warden. He told Maman to cover the windows with black paper so no light could be seen at night and that the gardener had been relocated to an internment camp. Oh, and also report any suspicious strangers to him at his address down the street.

America was at war! The Japs had bombed Pearl Harbor - when would they invade California?

It became clear that growing children were making it a necessity to buy a larger house. Maman had a knack for real estate and found a nicer, greener neighborhood in a northwesterly direction-a definite upgrade- a stucco and wooden English Tudor imitation on Dunsmuir Avenue. The movie industry had been the inspiration for local architects. To create copies of European mansions —French provincial, Spanish, Italian villas, Swiss chalets — often mixtures of facades that pleased, especially those who had never been to Europe but believed what the movies portrayed.

Papa wanted to live close to his business on Hollywood Boulevard allowing him to walk to work to avoid the long bus drive, so he sold the Dunsmuir house, and bought another home in the hills above Highland Avenue, not far from the famous Hollywood Bowl (this is an amphitheater in the Hollywood Hills neighborhood of Los Angeles, California, summer home of the Los Angeles Philharmonic since 1922).

.   When the family resided at 2020 Las Palmas Avenue, it was a quiet and safe neighborhood, the house roomy and comfortable except for the frequent shouting of their neighbors, the Gurdins, the parents of Natalie Wood, then known as Natasha (an American actress, she began her career in film as a child and became a successful Hollywood star as a young adult, receiving three Academy Award nominations before she turned 25 years old) . Little did Maria Gurdin know that Papa was fluent in Russian and cringed at some of the vulgarities, for Papa spoke a beautiful Czarist-Epoch Russian. Natasha's mother was known as an ambitious, fearless stage mother who made the round of the studios insisting her Natasha could play any role required, and she was obviously right.

Occasionally, we kids would speak in English at home, and Papa said "Parlez Francais."

Papa often held a dim view of everything French except the language, which he would not allow us to forget. This accounts for the fact that George and I speak French fluently. Many parents from Europe did not do that, and as a result their children could not speak their native language, which later on created a cultural distance between them.

The family settled into the pleasant war time life in Hollywood, with the big red street cars of Pacific Electric, whose express cars would swish you to the beach in Santa Monica in twenty minutes for a dime; the cinemas on Hollywood Boulevard for the Saturday afternoon kiddie crowd, featuring two second-run films - one major, one a "B" animated cartoon - a news reel and a short, all for a quarter, plus a nickel for popcorn. Life was sweet.

Lon McAllister, child actor, lived just a few doors away. You could run into Percy Kilbride (was an American character actor. He made a career of playing country hicks, most memorably as Pa Kettle in the *Ma and Pa Kettle* series of feature films), or Harry George Bryant Davenport (an American film and stage actor who worked in show business, playing Dr. Meade in the 1939 film *Gone with the Wind,* starting in films from the age of six (1872) until his death in 1949), wonderful character actors. One could also find a parking place on Hollywood Boulevard, even in front of the Egyptian theater (built in the 1920s by Sid Grauman, this pharaoh-themed theater screens rare, independent films and classic movies)!

Papa had his first shop right across the street from that famous landmark, and he was driven absolutely crazy by the monkeys that were lined up in cages on both sides of the long outdoor entrance to the theater. These little beasts would bang against their cages in perpetual motion and shriek as the tourists teased and fed them.

The traffic signals were highly legible signs, which alternated with the change of the lights: black on white GO when it was green and white on red STOP when it was red. To recollect the scene, one could

not say it was glamorous, but it was respectable, like the Hollywood
Roosevelt Hotel, across the street from Grauman's Chinese Theater
(now known as the TCL Chinese Theater, the building is a movie palace
on the historic Hollywood Walk of Fame at 6925 Hollywood Boulevard
in Hollywood, California) and of course the legendary Hollywood Hotel
at Highland and Hollywood Boulevard, the setting of a 1937 film
featuring Dick Powell (an American singer, actor, film producer, film
director and studio head. Though he came to stardom as a musical
comedy performer, he showed versatility and successfully transform
into leading male roles and first actor to portray the private detective
Philip Marlowe on screen), which launched the beloved song, *Hooray
for Hollywood.*

The 40's in America still very much belonged the era of immigrant
assimilation. We, the Du Bois children, were assimilating quite well. As
young children we naturally preferred the easy-goingness of our
American friends. We were given a minimum of toys, gadgets, clothes,
or money; rarely requesting anything, and looking back, we did not feel
deprived. It was pointed out to us that Papa worked hard to provide us
with a good home, proper food and an education. Papa always insisted
that life was serious and his children be prepared to face it. We gave the
impression of being more sophisticated, but in many ways were naive
and were not taught to value kids our own age as well as the families
they came from.

By 1944, we had moved to a two-story house. The family was told
Jean Harlow (she was most famous American film actress and sex
symbol of the 1930s. Jean Harlow was signed by director Howard

Hughes, and her first major appearance was in *Hell's Angels*, known as the "Blonde Bombshell",) had lived there, in the fashionable Whitley Heights in the Hollywood Hills. Papa owned a 1941 Buick convertible, which was rarely out of the two-car garage at 6611 Emmett Terrace. Southern California is and was the most automobile driven place on earth, and yet Papa would not use his car and would walk to work and back, a good five miles one way. Maman finally explained that when Papa was a young man, he was an eager motorcyclist. He was riding his vehicle on some European cornice when suddenly, on a blind turn, a bus loaded with passengers rolled down a steep ravine to avoid the young motorcyclist. A terrible guilt prevented him from wanting to operate any vehicle for the rest of his life. Maman, who had been chauffeured before marrying, had no interest in driving and I decided not to drive as well. The family lived way up in the hills and no one drove. It was odd, but one gets used to oddities.

It was a golden age of street vendors who went from neighborhood to neighborhood selling their wares. The Helms man with his assortment of bakery goods, the beloved and never to be forgotten Good Humor man (selling ice cream), and then of course the tinkers, mobile knife sharpeners, and others.

In those days, fathers were the figure of authority, since fathers were rarely home as they were the breadwinners. When Papa put in a long day as a self-employed shopkeeper, no one in the family ever doubted or ever needed to know how he was spending his time. He had only one vice, light gambling, never discussed at home. Years later he took his eldest son to accompany him to the office of the E.F. Hutton &

Company stock exchange at the crack of dawn, but gave not one word of any information about the stock market as if it was some sort of addiction to be avoided.

It is only natural when you first begin to live every day in a new location, new culture, an unfamiliar language, no help from servants, strange foods, and other peculiarities, to have a tendency to jump to conclusions and be absolutely convinced that anything European is the gold standard. Maman could go to Safeway and fill her grocery bag with a dollar that 65 years later would require about $15.

On August 15th, 1945 the war was over and V-J day (Victory over Japan) was declared. Some sailors had grabbed giggling girls and pulled them on top of the red street cars, yelling and waving to celebrate the end of the bloodiest massacre in human history. Every morning one of these street cars known jokingly as the "Slave Wagon" left from the negro community of Watts filled with domestic servants, dropped them off at different points where they would be picked up by their employers and then return them to the Santa Monica Boulevard drop-off for the journey, except for Harriet, who worked for our family. She had to trudge up the hill and screamed with delight, "Hallelujah, and thanks be to de Laud."

Blessed Sacrament, Youri's Catholic school, felt it was a monumental struggle of good vs. evil, and God was on our side. They had the taste and the wisdom not to mention that a lot of Germans were Catholic and many Russians were atheists.

The five years following the end of the war, prosperity reigned. The seducer of the era was black and white television. Papa, who worked six days a week, buying and selling collections and later war souvenirs and coins, was sad when soldiers sold their Purple Hearts, but realized they needed the money.

For the family, 1950 started with a bang. On January 1st, it snowed in Hollywood, an extremely rare occurrence. On that very morning, Papa was held up at gunpoint, ordered to unlock his safe and surrender its contents, estimated to be worth $50,000 - a fortune at that time, his life's work. One can't help wondering about the wisdom of locking valuables in a safe where thieves close to the victim usually are aware of the nature of the loot. Also, valuable stamps are almost impossible to inventory. At their true value for insurance purposes (they are continually being bought and sold, then there is the IRS) and that type of insurance is prohibitive - a total loss. Papa was extremely resilient, and went to work the next day. They never caught the robbers.

Myself with Ralph Bellamy at Universal Studios in 1942

Chapter 3

A Star Is Born?

The Hollywood fantasy started early for me at the age of six. While I was attending a ballet class, a top children's agent, Lola Moore, who often scoured children's classes of all sorts hoping to find new talent, talked to my mother and told her that Universal was searching for a six-year-old girl who spoke French to do a leading role in a picture called *Journey for Margaret.* Maman agreed, and I was taken to the interview. The men in charge took an instant liking to me and all agreed that I was perfect for the role — then destiny stepped in. Ralph Bellamy (a famous American actor whose career spanned 62 years on stage, screen and television,) who was shooting *The Great Impersonator* on a nearby set, came to visit. He was wearing an intimidating black uniform with menacing boots, a swastika armband and leather holster with pistol. The studio immediately had him take my hand and started taking a series of photos. I had the impression of being led to my execution. I had been traumatized by the many swastikas and Nazis I had seen before and was frightened.

I screamed in a loud voice, "I WILL NOT WORK WITH A NAZI!"

They tried to persuade me but to no avail. Finally the studio could not risk working with a hysterical child. Maman did not to try to influence me as she knew nothing of the motion picture business and thought it was not very important anyway. *A Star is Born* – but it wasn't me. Margret O'Brien excelled in the role of child star. (Margaret was an American film, radio, television, and stage actress. She began a prolific career at the age of four as a child actress in feature films for Metro-Goldwyn-Mayer Studios. She became one of the most popular child stars in cinema history and was honored with a Juvenile Academy Award as the outstanding child actress of 1944, later in her career she appeared on television, on stage, and in supporting film roles).

Soon afterwards I was cast as one of the refugee children in *The Amazing Mrs. Holiday*, starring Deanna Durbin (she was a Canadian-born actress and singer, later settled in France, who appeared in musical films in the 1930s and 1940) and Edmund O'Brien (an American actor who appeared in more than 100 films from the 1940s to the 1970s, often playing character parts). This particular picture lasted six months because of a change in directors. I attended school, which was set-up in the studio, but had plenty of free time because of the elaborate lighting for the film. In those days lighting took up most of the time.

One of my unforgettable moments happened while I was playing with the other children in the back lot between scenes. I was impressed by the magnificent structures that were erected on the fake green rolling hills. However, I came to discover after exploring these mansions, stores, buildings, and barns, that they were actually a Potemkin village - elaborate phony facade held up by planks of construction lumber. It made an indelible impression on the way I would view life, to examine things behind the scenes, never quite trusting my first impressions.

I remember sitting next to Boris Karloff (his real name was William Henry Pratt, better known by his stage name of Boris Karloff, he was an English actor who was primarily known for his roles in horror films. He portrayed Frankenstein's monster in *Frankenstein, Bride of Frankenstein* and *The Son of Frankenstein*) my jaw dropped watching him in his Frankenstein outfit while he was adjusting a screw on his green neck; I stared and he winked. So much for horror pictures. I asked a waiting father, who had two children in the film and had to be there every day, as did my mother (I thought it must be hard on his work, thinking of my own father).

I asked him with an innocence that wasn't meant to be rude, "What do you do for a living?"

"I manage my children."

"No, no, I mean to earn money."

He laughed and repeated, "I manage my children."

I wondered why he doesn't answer me?

I told Maman, who said, "Oh no, you didn't say that!"

The days were long and most of the time one waited between takes. On this day there was a group of Chinese soldiers huddled together for a scene and I asked if I could sit on one of their laps. I talked and laughed easily with them. The following day the scene still had not been shot and I looked for my lap of the previous day, going from one to the other.

"Are you the one I sat on yesterday? You all look so much the same."

They all laughed, no one had heard of political correctness in those days.

Another thing that baffled me was the fascination that the children shared for collecting the stars' autographs.

I asked them, "But why? We see them every day."

As a child, I was gregarious and could hold my own with all types of kids, younger or older, but was reluctant to learn lines and read for casting personnel. I seemed to lack the self-confidence that was needed. Maman was a fairly indifferent mother at the studio, not at home. Still basically formed by the European upbringing of the era that show business was a little on the vulgar side, although my parents were grateful for the money that it brought. When groups of children were called for an interview, I hid behind them hoping to be invisible, but they seemed to want me even more.

Once at Warner Brothers Studios, I was asked to repeat lines read to me in a dull monotone. I repeated them exactly as I heard them; I didn't get the role. The studio had a policy of giving a child fifty cents if they did not get the role.

My eyes lit up. "Thank God, I didn't get the role."

Maman said, "That's not necessary."

In a film with Barbara Britton (she was an American film and television actress. Best known for her Western film roles opposite Randolph Scott (film career spanned from 1928 to 1962, best known for being tall-in-the-saddle, Western Hero), Joel McCrea (an American actor whose career spanned almost five decades and appearances in more than 90 films, including Alfred Hitchcock's spy film *Foreign Correspondent* and Preston Sturges' comedy classic *Sullivan's Travels* 1940), mostly Western film roles from 1946 to her retirement in 1976), and Gene Autry (another Western film actor and singer). Barbara Britton was also known for her two-year tenure as inquisitive amateur sleuth Pam North on the television and radio series *Mr. and Mrs. North.*) I was wearing a white communion dress. As usual I was hiding behind a bush, and a pigeon did his business on me. Everyone told me it would bring me good luck. And it did, because I immediately got a part in a movie called *Dark Waters* with Merle Oberon (she was an Anglo-Indian actress. She began her film career in British films as Anne Boleyn in *The Private Life of Henry VIII.* After her success in *The Scarlet Pimpernel*, she travelled to the United States to make films for Samuel Goldwyn) and Franchot Tone (Stanislaus Pascal Franchot Tone, was an American stage, film, and television actor. He is perhaps best known for his Oscar nominated role as Midshipman Roger Byam in *Mutiny on the Bounty*, starring alongside Clark Gable (William Clark Gable was an American film actor and military officer, often referred to as "The King of Hollywood" or just simply as "The King") and Charles Laughton (he was an English stage and film actor, director, producer and screenwriter. Laughton was trained in London at the Royal

Academy of Dramatic Art and first appeared professionally on the stage in 1926). At this point there were many opportunities for children in these war-time productions and a future career might have been had. I did appear briefly in a few films, but I lacked a combination of ambition, desire, and energy for a career.

My brother Jean Jacques appeared in one movie with Paul Henried (he was an Austrian-born American actor and film director. He is best remembered for two timeless roles: as Victor Laszlo in *Casablanca* and as Jerry Durrance in *Now, Voyager,* both released in 1942. He also appeared with Hedy Lamarr in *Conspirators* (she was an Austrian-born American film actress and inventor. After a brief early film career in Czechoslovakia, including the controversial *Ecstasy* in which she is seen swimming and running in the nude. She became a film star with MGM from the 1930s to the 1950s after being signed by Louis B. Meyer in Paris, France). Jean Jacques appeared in *The Conspirators.*

His memorable line was, "Look, Mommy, lights, lights!"

I actually worked enough hours so that when I was not working, I received a hefty twenty-five dollars a week for unemployment, the full salary of many a breadwinner. Jean Jacques and I went to Selma Avenue Grammar School in Hollywood. I didn't realize I was nearsighted until one day the school tested me and told me to get glasses, which I did, but never wore them. I squinted my way through school. I was not an impressive student, but learned to read almost overnight. Youri went to the Blessed Sacrament, a Catholic school across the street, because our parents felt he was gifted and it was worth the money.

I went on to LeConte Junior High, where my closest friend there, Ann Carter, had an impressive career as a child actress (was an American child actress, who worked with dozens of film stars, compiling an "unimaginably distinguished résumé" despite an acting career which lasted only slightly more than a decade). At age six, she starred as Veronica Lake's daughter in *I Married a Witch*. Ann was a beautiful little girl with large gray eyes and long blonde hair. She starred in *Curse of the Cat People* and had many other credits to her name. They named her the golden child. She was very talented, had no inhibitions in front of the camera and had a very focused mother on her side. I was happy with that friendship, as I wasn't particularly popular with many kids.

At home, where only French was spoken, I was often told, "Don't be vulgar, or don't be American," meaning anything my parents objected to, which made me feel superior and inadequate at the same time, a queer duck. Papa was tight with money and I didn't have fashionable clothes. I never wore makeup, didn't own a purse, had no money, and criticized the school's food, bad manners, etc. Who did I think I was? Other than Ann, I made friends with a homely girl whose mother used to beat her because she wasn't beautiful like her older sister. I used to preach to her and told her not to put up with the abuse. I also made friends with some black kids. I wondered why blacks and whites didn't mix more. On a very dark night two black boys from school came to visit, one tall, one short. Maman open the door and saw four eyeballs looking at her, and she screamed.

Meanwhile George (English for Youri), who condensed four years of high school into two in a private school, the Marian Colbert School of Individual Instruction, graduated at fifteen and went on to University of California, Los Angeles (UCLA). He had a guru-like quality and had a following of men, all older, who treated him as if he were an oracle. I was eleven and George's friends treated me like a sister, taking me to the beach, movies, and the Hollywood Bowl (The Hollywood Bowl is an amphitheater in the Hollywood Hills neighborhood of Los Angeles, California). I felt at ease, comfortable, and loved to talk to them. By the time I was fifteen and developed an hourglass figure – 36, 23, 36 – I was comfortable and happy with all the attention. There was rivalry and complaints among George's friends, and George got bored listening to them complaining about his sister.

I graduated junior high and went to Hollywood High. I lost my friend Ann Carter as Ann moved. Papa had his business two blocks from Hollywood High, and I would always go and check in and kiss him, as did my brother Jean Jacques. Papa's customers were amused, as American children didn't kiss their parents, it wasn't a custom.

I found out that there existed a school for children that worked for the movies. MGM chief Louis B. Mayer asked a Mrs. Bertha Mann (American film and stage actress) to open a professional school for child actors to accommodate their working hours, so that's how Hollywood Professional School (HPS) came into being. After a year at Hollywood High School, my parents agreed to enroll me in HPS. In the past it had a tremendous reputation. I was hoping to start a movie career as I was constantly being approached by agents about a career in movies. HPS had opened in 1935 and apparently half of Hollywood had gone there. At the age of fifteen I made the move. HPS was located at the corner of Gower and Hollywood Boulevard in Los Angeles, in what had once upon a time been an impressive building, and was now rather dilapidated in my eyes. The science class had several explosions that had never been repaired.

The first day I went, a fellow student told me no one attends the first day of school, so we went to play miniature golf. The roll call was very slack and no one commented about my absences. I had never been in a school like this. One day, in English class the teacher came in quite tipsy, recited a poem and left. I was told this was not unusual. I never told my parents about the school. Part of me wished my parents took a bigger part in my education and guided me. I knew the school was not run properly, the other part of me was delighted. Maman had so much structure and instruction when she was young, she loved giving people what she called freedom. Papa on the other hand was too strict, but didn't think my education mattered. Two grown men had already asked him for my hand in marriage. He told me about this later.

"Why didn't you tell me?" I asked.

"You were too young." He'd already had to deal with his crazy sister.

The hours varied for many of the students because of their working schedule, so I never knew who was in school, although I recall some of my classmates: Lisa Gaye, Debra Paget's sister (Debra Paget is an American actress and entertainer. She is perhaps best known for her performances in Cecil B. DeMille's epic *The Ten Commandments* and in *Love Me Tender,* and for the risqué snake dance scene in *The Indian*

Tomb). Venetia Stevenson (director Robert Stevenson's daughter) (she is an English-American film and television actress), Jimmy Devon Boyd was an American singer, musician of *I Saw Mommy Kissing Santa Claus* fame. I wasn't working so I had regular school hours. I saw many beautiful girls getting picked up in limousines. A friend of George's, who was considered brilliant by George, and his entourage, used to walk with me and talk with me about philosophical things. He gave me a book on Plato, then he sent me love letters, which I immediately showed George and his friends. I could hardly contain myself. Did that mean I was intelligent? I always had doubts as my brother was gifted mentally. The friend told me that he was disappointed in me. I was extraordinarily embarrassed. I stared myself in the mirror and thought about the effect I had on men and made a monumental decision. I could always read Plato later, (the philosopher in Classical Greece and the founder of the Academy in Athens, the first institution of higher learning in the Western world.) This was the time for living.

Another friend of George's had me pinned down on the floor of a car, claiming he was exercising his constitutional rights to pursue happiness. I laughed so hard, he stopped. Perhaps because I had two brothers, I was never angry but rather sympathetic to the plight of men. After all, the male had to make advances, but one could say no kindly.

At fifteen I attended Caroline Leonetti's School of Charm on Sunset Boulevard in Hollywood (Caroline Leonetti Ahmanson was an American fashion consultant, businesswoman and philanthropist. She was a corporate director of The Walt Disney Company and the Fluor Corporation), thinking I could model, but I was five foot four – I was offered pin-ups and nudes.

Caroline Leonetti used to make an occasional speech to the girls: "Accentuate the positive and eliminate the negative."

She went on to marry Howard Ahmanson, who built Home Savings & Loan, so it must have worked.

And then there was Mrs. Tex Ritter (movie actress "cowgirl" of the 1930s, wife of the singer Tex Ritter), John Ritter's mother, who held a class on how to catch a man. If your man likes fishing, learn every detail about it, even if you hate it.

"Do you have to live that lie the rest of your life?" I asked.

"Oh no, just to get him." It was a quaint idea.

Muriel Donnellan, a well-known harpist who performed in the orchestra of the film studios and at the Hollywood Bowl, who had many theatrical friends, became one of Maman's closest friends. When I turned sixteen, I went to a party hosted by Muriel, where I met a handsome English actor Robin Hughes (he was a British film and television actor). One of Robin's movies was *Auntie Mame.* He was the rogue who impregnated Mame's secretary. He was six foot two, blonde, and 32. He called the next day and asked if I could come ice-skating. I did not date any boys in school, although now they were paying a great deal of attention to me. This was my cup of tea. I didn't know how to skate, but I liked the attention from such an attractive man. I could carry on a conversation and did not sound like a teenager, as I was used to talking to much to older people. We went ice-skating for the better part of six months, much to my dismay, as I didn't like skating. Robin took me to meet many of his actor friends, most of them older than Robin. One was Colonel Ramsey Hill, who had been in the Bengal Lancers (numerous regiments of British Indian Army) and always assumed a pose he called the cavalry stance. He explained that his feet just naturally fell into that position. At one gathering, a friend asked him why his wife left him.

"I never really knew," he replied. When asked, "Wasn't it because she caught you in the bathtub with a blonde?"

He said, "Oh, you know about that, huh?"

I loved all the funny bitchy stories and attitudes, and of course there were the tragedies. Ramsey had sent his only son John off to an exclusive, costly prep school back east. The other boys were from wealthy families. Ramsey, apart from being very frugal (or for a better word, tight), thought it didn't build character. After repeated requests for money, John took the gun his father had given him as a present and shot himself in the head at the age of seventeen while on the phone with his father.

Another well-known English character actor, John Abbott, who gave pleasant parties, and who was decidedly gay and very charming.

He said to Maman about Robin's fascination with me, "Well, who wouldn't want a lovely sixteen-year-old virgin?"

John Abbott became a good friend to the Du Bois household.

Robin got the lead role in Robert Sherwood's *The Road to Rome,* presented and directed by the very famous Hollywood director Preston Sturges in his theater restaurant, "The Players," on the Sunset Strip, right next to the Chateau Marmont. It could have been called "The Road to Ruin" for Sturges, but that's another story. Preston Sturges had been one of Hollywood's most highly regarded and highly paid writer and director. In the talkies, he was the first writer to become a director and the first to direct his own script. He won the first Academy Award for Best Original Screenplay for the film *The Great McGinty,* his first of three nominations in the category. His comedies were considered incomparable. It was summer vacation and Robin brought me to the rehearsals as much as I could get away. There I met the larger than life Preston Sturges, who repeatedly told me how much I looked like Claudette Colbert (she was an American stage and film actress and a leading lady in Hollywood for over two decades, and has been called "The mixture of inimitable beauty, sophistication, wit, and vivacity,") whom he had directed in several movies. Quite a compliment!

Caroline Jones was the leading lady. She was accompanied by what I thought was an odd looking man with a protruding Adam's apple and large bulging eyes, Aaron Spelling (he was an American film and television producer. Some of his successes include the TV programs *Charlie's Angels, The Love Boat, Dynasty, Beverly Hills, 90210, 7th Heaven,* and *Charmed*). Caroline Jones was married to Aaron Spelling from 1953 to 1964. Usually he was seen with a script under his arm and pipe in his mouth. Caroline Jones looked impressive on stage, but odd backstage. I thought, in my nearly seventeen years of wisdom, how cruel life was, that these odd-looking but hard working people hoped to succeed in Hollywood. I spent several weeks backstage with Ms. Jones, who was very pleasant with me.

Although later, when I appeared in a TV show with her, I immediately said, "It's so good to see you. How are you?"

She stared blankly and said, "I'm sorry, I don't remember you," as did Aaron Spelling, when I was waiting to read for a part.

Spelling came in – "Where have you been all my life?" – as a greeting, and then said that he didn't know me.

Maybe he remembered the time Keith (my soon-to-be boyfriend) and Sturges had been sitting drinking, both rather tipsy.

Keith said to Preston, "Look at that wanker" – meaning Spelling – which he couldn't help but overhear.

I'm sure that didn't help, even though Keith profusely apologized the next day. I decided many people don't want to be reminded of their early days.

Keith McConnell, an Irish actor, was cast in a supporting role. Maman who accompanied me on occasion, was talking to Sturges.

"Now there's an elegant man," pointing to Keith. She was to rue the day.

When I was introduced to Keith, it was instantaneous combustion. We both came from upper middle class backgrounds; it was like a reenactment of a 1930's movie. The setting was the theater restaurant; Preston Sturges' presence was very imposing, the very glamorous Keith, and Maman's approval.

Sturges and Maman were speaking French, and he told her, "Oh, I hear your Belgian accent."

She immediately snapped back, "How would you know?"

Maman had absolutely no reverence for the movie industry; just for class and that there was only one way to speak French. The repartee was funny and witty, always of course at the expense of anyone they didn't feel was their equal or beautiful.

Preston, demanding one whiskey sour after another, and Keith easily drank his share. The evenings seemed magical, this was the Hollywood everyone expected and few experienced. Preston held court and many interesting and famous people came by.

One night, author William Faulkner came in (William Cuthbert Faulkner was an American writer and Nobel Prize laureate from Oxford, Mississippi. Faulkner wrote novels, short stories, a play, poetry, essays, and screenplays,) which led to the ever sarcastic Sturges to comment, "He has just been awarded a Pulitzer prize and he's only five foot two."

Keith laughed as did others.

I thought, is that really kind, and then didn't think about it at all. Keith, at the age of twenty eight, perfectly groomed and immaculately tailored down to his custom-made shoes, was charming and witty with the proper upper class accent; but had an Irish mischievousness and warmth, not often found in the more pompous English actors of that era. Keith invited me for lunch at Paramount Studios where he was filming by day, and at night, in the play.

The main fare of early TV was 1930's movies. I adored that era of clothes; the way men looked and spoke, the beautiful interiors with winding staircases, and especially the conversations. I felt when I grew up, that was the life I wanted, not white picket fences. Keith was that and more. Robin was very unhappy; he told me he wanted to marry me. I felt depressed and I also felt much too young. I told Robin I had to experience life, hadn't he? He agreed and said he would wait until I had made up my mind. I had, but didn't want to hurt him. Fortunately, we had not consummated our relationship. Robin had a lot of women, wondering when he would come to his senses. He was very sought after by women and not long after, he impregnated an actress who sued him; it was in the papers. It made an easy excuse for me to break it off. John Carradine, a character actor, (John Carradine was an American actor, best known for his roles in horror films, Westerns, and Shakespearean theater) who was a close friend of Robin's, told him to be patient, that I would forgive him - after all this is Hollywood. That cast and others were amused; often making malicious comments about two adult males fighting over such a young girl. Unfortunately, I could no longer go to the Players, as I was seeing Keith and there was too much tension between Keith and Robin. I missed it, but I had chosen Keith and that was that.

I was able to graduate from HPS, at seventeen; partially I thought because Robin had done a lot of my homework, or the complete indifference at the school and bad situation to detail by the school or a bit of both. HPS closed in 1984 due to lack of enrollment. Keith and Maman were at my graduation where I recited some poetry in French. I thought I was very mediocre as my stage fright kicked in, but it seemed to satisfy.

I went to City College to study drama. The drama teacher started to pursue me and after six months I left. Perhaps I didn't like the repetitive word or wasn't interested. At this time I lived at home but spent most of my time with Keith, which made my parents very unhappy. Papa decided to make the best of it, knowing you can't do much about love, and offered to buy a gas station for Keith; in those days it was not a fortune. He thought of all of Keith's cars and thought it was a good combination. Keith was taken back with the idea. He? The owner of a gas station? God Forbid! He didn't come all the way to America to own a gas station.

Barry Fitzgerald (above, center left) Deanna Durbin (standing in rear) and myself (center) in the 1942 Universal production of "Forever Yours"

Barry Fitzgerald, Deanna Durbin and myself (center right) in the 1942 Universal production of "Forever Yours"

Teddy Infer and me (right) with Deanna Durbin in "Forever Yours" 1942

Birthday party on the set of "Forever Yours".
Deanna Durbin (center) and me on the shoulders of Edmond O'Brien

A gathering of all the children with Harry Davenport
on the set of 'Forever Yours" 1942

Chapter 4

Luck of the Irish

Keith McConnell came from an affluent family. Born in Dublin, Ireland in 1923, his father was a famous soccer and golfing champion in his own country. Keith's parents were youthful and striking, which in that era didn't suit his more conservative older brother Paul, and his sister Patricia. It was a source of embarrassment when they came to the school functions where they stood out from the other parents. Not Keith – he relished it! His father had an import export business and his Uncle owned McConnell's advertising in Dublin. Keith and his family lived in an upscale neighborhood in Monkstown, in a large Georgian house.

Keith was asthmatic as a child, and his very eccentric mother kept him home from school. Later his parents sent him to the very prestigious West of England Public School "Downside." Keith had the distinction of being the last boy to be publicly flogged for having sex with one of the school's maids. It was very difficult for Keith in that very British school as he was fiercely patriotic about Ireland. He studied Economics at Trinity College and then joined the Irish army where he became a Corporal.

Michael O'Herlihy, who later became a director in Hollywood, was also an Irish actor, (he was an Irish television producer and director who directed shows like *Gunsmoke, Maverick, Star Trek, Hawaii Five-O, M*A*S*H* and *The A-Team*. Born in Dublin, Ireland, O'Herlihy was the younger brother of actor Dan O'Herlihy. (Daniel Peter O'Herlihy was an Irish-born film actor, known for such roles as Brigadier General Warren A. "Blackie" Black in *Fail Safe,* Conal Cochran in *Halloween III: Season of the Witch,* "The Old Man" in *RoboCop,* and Andrew Packard in *Twin Peaks*). Dan O'Herlihy's brother said that Keith was the only Corporal who had his uniform tailor-made. The Irish poked fun at each other. Ridicule was in their blood, not unlike the French. Keith's brother, Paul, joined the British army and became a Colonel. He led a very successful campaign in the Persian Gulf (part of the Indian Ocean in Western Asia.) "Let's face it," he told Keith, "the British are the salt of the Earth," which made Keith livid as he viewed the English as "800 years of fearful oppression." Keith was six foot two, blonde, with large blue eyes, long lashes, an aquiline face, and an infectious grin. He had a very athletic figure like Tarzan (Johnny Weissmuller was an Austro-Hungarian-born American competition swimmer and actor, best known for playing Tarzan in films

of the 1930s and 1940s and for having one of the best competitive
swimming records of the 20th century). Keith made a dashing
appearance, wore all his custom-made clothes to perfection. Many
considered him haughty, which was not the case. He was a very warm,
down-to-earth person with a tremendous sense of humor and a huge
heart. Ask him for help and he'd always come through. He adored
beauty and glamour, so when he met the very famous (or infamous)
Jack Doyle, (Joseph "Jack" Doyle, known as "The Gorgeous Gael", was
an Irish boxer, actor and a tenor. He was born Joseph Doyle and known
to his friends as Joe but changed it to Jack when starting his professional
career) and Movita at their night club "The Swizzle Stick" in London, it
was a perfect fit.

Doyle had also been in the Irish army earlier and had been the boxing
champion of the Irish army. Doyle became an international boxing
legend. He had the right hook of Jack Dempsey (William Harrison
"Jack" Dempsey, nicknamed "Kid Blackie" and "The Manassa Mauler",
was an American professional boxer who competed from 1914 to 1927,
and reigned as the world heavyweight champion from 1919 to 1926).
Doyle had a beautiful tenor voice, was six foot five, and looked like
Tyrone Power (Tyrone Edmund Power III was an American film, stage
and radio actor. From the 1930s to the 1950s, Power appeared in dozens
of films, often in swashbuckler roles or romantic leads . Doyle was
nicknamed "The Gorgeous Gael." He was the darling of high society
and the Royals. He was considered a phenomenon in the boxing world.
Women fell over themselves. He had an affect very much like a rock
star of today. When Doyle met Movita, she had broken a date with

Howard Hughes to be with him. It was beauty meeting gorgeous. When Jack asked Movita to marry him three days later, she left her career to be with this incredible man. She had been in *Flying Down to Rio*. Many thought she was even more beautiful than its star, Dolores Del Rio (she was a Mexican actress. She was the first major female Latin American crossover star in Hollywood, with a career in American films in the 1920s and 1930s). Movita also had a lovely soprano voice. She was cast in the original *Mutiny on the Bounty* as Franchot Tone's love interest. She did several independent movies in which she starred, some with John Carroll (an American actor and singer). She gave up a promising career for Doyle. When he met them, Keith thought this was the world I want to be part of – Irish wit and charm, glamour, exceptional beauty, adoration. It was so natural for them to be close friends. Keith's family did not approve of their son's association with the Doyles thinking it would be scandalous. Doyle's notoriety was flagrant, yet it probably secretly impressed them, like so many people are with the rich and famous. There was no stopping Keith and his association with the Doyles.

The Irish culture is steeped in alcohol, and the people are very tolerant of drinking, even to excess, but as time went on, Doyle's drinking became intolerable. At this time, Movita and Jack were touring Europe, singing together. Movita had to cover for Jack because of the drinking. She was becoming very popular with the audiences because of her beauty and voice. To be fair to Jack Doyle, a book of his life was written in 1990, *Fighting For Love* by Michael Taub, and gives the full story of this unusual man.

Jack lashed out at Movita and became physically abusive. He destroyed his boxing career, singing career, and marriage. Keith's nature was that of a rescuer, apart for his increased feelings for Movita. Movita had a series of commitments and contracts, but she felt it was not prudent to stay any longer, and she wanted to return to the U.S. Keith was good at negotiating and helped her get her affairs in order and leave.

Keith was drawn to acting; it seemed like second nature with his movie star appearance and presence. He went to London where he had friends and ending up working and got some very useful experience. Had he stayed he might have had a good career, but he wanted to go to Hollywood where they made the movies of his childhood, and there was Movita. He arrived a couple of years later in New York at the Waldorf Astoria, where he put his hand-made shoes outside his room, where he expected them to be cleaned and returned. They never were to be seen again. He had also packed a cape and a top hat. Too many Fred Astaire movies, (Fred Astaire was an American dancer, singer, actor, choreographer and television presenter. He is widely regarded as one of the most influential dancers in the history of film and television musicals!) He was having his shoes shined in a shoeshine stand when the man next to him put both fingers in his ears and wiggled them. Keith thought the man must be touched, pretending not to notice. After a while he peered again and the man repeated the gesture.

"Aren't you an elk?" the man then said, pointing to Keith's family crest ring where there was a prominent elk.

Keith had many letters of introduction from English friends at the studios; he was greeted by various agents who in turn introduced him to the beautiful people - women, models, and actresses. Later he explained to me that he was not prepared for the cultural clash. He would invite a model or an actress to dinner, she would order the most expensive thing on the menu and barely eat it, which to Keith seemed unpardonable.

With very little ceremony some of the ladies would say, "Let's go fuck." Keith, suave Keith, was surprised.

His destination was Hollywood and Movita.

When he arrived in Hollywood, he immediately went to see Movita, who was living in the Silver Lake District, where the Mexican colony lived and many still do. Keith was in love, Movita was happy to see him. They lived together for three years in West Hollywood on Harper Avenue in a beautiful Spanish building, Harper House. Movita, who had left Hollywood right when she was very much in demand to marry Jack Doyle and then fled Europe from another very promising career to get away from him, was downsizing her career. She was a Latin actress, and the U.S. had somewhat lost its interest in Latin actresses at that time.

Keith landed a leading role in a series, the remake of *Topper*, starring Leon Errol. The first day of filming, Leon dropped dead. This was a glimpse into the future that would plague Keith. Financially, the couple was struggling. Movita was used to attention and a very lavish lifestyle. Keith's upper class attitude kept him from being depressed as he felt his lack of money was not who he was. Movita was offered a small part in the movie *Viva Zapata*, to be filmed in Mexico. She went to Mexico and met Marlon Brando, (Marlon Brando was an American actor and film director. He is credited with bringing realism to film acting, helping to popularize the Stanislavski system of acting, studying with Stella Adler in the 1940s.) Movita was eight years older than Brando and Keith, but her beauty was ageless. Brando was smitten; Keith was devastated, but strangely happy for her. She might have everything she wanted and needed.

Keith was not having a successful career; he should have stayed in London. The haughty refined English type was not in style. Keith was entrepreneurial by nature; he tried to import Mezcal from Mexico, but the authorities said it had a dead worm in it so they did not allow it. He then bought three used cars, had them painted green and white and labeled Sunset Cab Company. Keith had only his Irish driver's license and no insurance; he hired two drivers and at times drove one of the cars himself. Keith dropped off a customer at "The Players." Preston Sturges took an instant liking to this crazy Irishman. As they talked, Keith told him about the cabs and Preston told Keith he could park his cars permanently in front of his restaurant in the parking lot. He immediately cast him in his upcoming production of *The Road to Rome.*

One night Keith was driving Peter O'Toole (Peter Seamus O'Toole was a British stage and film actor of Irish descent. He attended the Royal Academy of Dramatic Art and began working in the theater, gaining recognition as a Shakespearean actor, starred in *Lawrence of Arabia* (1962) for which he received his first nomination for the Academy Award for Best Actor. He was nominated for this award another seven times – for *Becket (1964), The Lion in Winter (1968), Goodbye, Mr. Chips"(1969), The Ruling Class (1972), The Stunt Man*

(1980), My Favorite Year (1982), and *Venus (*2006) – and holds the record for the most Academy Award nominations for acting without a win) and Robert Newton (Robert Guy Newton was an English stage and film actor. Along with Errol Flynn, Newton was one of the most popular actors among the male juvenile audience of the 1940s and early 1950s, especially with British boys) , all three of them drunk as skunks. Keith seemed to walk on water, he was never stopped. The Yellow Cab Company, which had a virtual monopoly, was very unhappy and beat up one of Keith's drivers. Keith finally called it quits as it was less dangerous and more promising to be a star. Sturges told Keith that this was in his future, he would see to it.

One night renowned English actor Robert Newton, the original pirate *Long John Silver,* put his head under a woman's skirt, exclaiming, "I'm an old fashioned photographer!"

One day, Keith and I were having tea with Bobby Newton, as his friends called him.

"I can't understand how the queen won't invite me for tea," he said.

After all he was considered one of the great English actors, never mind the drinking. Keith had worked with him in London and said he was very kind. Keith adored amusing antics, I just adored Keith, Now that he was alone, Keith made a decision to move from his lovely Harper House apartment to a forty dollar a month walk-up flat above a shop on a tacky section of Santa Monica Boulevard and Fairfax Avenue. Art Peters, one of the drivers of his now defunct cab company (Peters acted like a valet, without the uniform), painted the apartment a dark hunter green with white molding and Art Peters, thinking to please his majesty, painted all the many pipes in gold.

Keith gasped, yelled, then recovered his sense of humor and said, "Quick! Repaint them white!"

In this shabby apartment, he put his Georgian silver, which he had brought from Ireland. The refrigerator emitted shocks when you touched it - you could say grandeur met poverty.

There was good news, or so it seemed. Katharine Hepburn (Katharine Houghton Hepburn was an American actress. Known for her fierce independence and spirited personality, Hepburn was a leading lady in Hollywood for more than 60 years) had acquired the rights to George Bernard Shaw's *The Millionaires* and wanted Sturges to direct. Sturges thought Keith would be perfect opposite Hepburn and sent Keith to New York for Hepburn's approval. She approved, but it was Sturges who was rejected by the producers. Sturges' last two films bombed. Another failure for Keith, who also did the last cigarette ad for *Tareyton Cigarettes*. They had Keith use his own Rolls Royce. The day after filming, those who decide explained that cigarettes were no longer to be advertised on TV. As for Sturges (his mother was Irish), he closed his restaurant and moved to New York where Sandy, his wife, who remained a friend of ours, told Keith and me that Preston went to see his doctor for a personal check-up.

Preston called Sandy to say, "All is well, I'm coming home," went to the elevator and dropped dead.

Myself behind the stairs in the United Artist's release of Dark Waters *with Merle Oberon and Franchot Tone 1944*

Diane Du Bois, Hawaiian publicity shot

Chapter 5

The Odd Couple

The Odd Couple seemed like an appropriate title; but when one thinks about it, every couple is odd, they're just not aware of it. They say women like bad boys, but I loved Keith because of his extreme empathy for people. I realize now of his great need to be loved. I dismissed the side I didn't approve of, as a "crazy wild Irishman." This satisfied my ego. How could I be associated with anything less than incredible?

When I first saw Keith's apartment, all I saw was the elegant man with his impeccable suits and his vibrant personality. I quickly removed all the doilies that some well-meaning girl had put there. I cleaned and polished all his remarkable Georgian silver. As we got closer, I asked him to remove Motiva's portrait from above his bed, which was hard for him to do as he liked to hold on to everything and everyone.

Having given up his taxi company, he had purchased several cars. From the day he arrived in the late 40's, he was almost as attracted to elegant cars as he was to what the Irish call a jar (a drink). Among his collection was a lovely green Mark-V Jaguar, three 1949 Lincoln Continentals, one in green, one in burgundy, and one in black, and a

1952 Mercedes 300 S. Later he added a Rolls Royce. All cars were convertibles. He would rent out these cars to working actors at a reasonable rate; he was definitely an entrepreneur, but he was too generous and not a businessman. Many actors owed him money, and these delicate autos were almost never serviced for oil and water, and the gas was never replaced. Keith and I were constantly out of gas or in a mechanic's shop; once the kind driver of a bus pushed us. Between the glamorous cars and Keith's magnificent wardrobe, everything was initialed, even his silk underwear, and even with the dreadful apartment, I was happy with this bizarre creature. Keith was happy because I created a sensation with my pinup figure, almost as good as an impressive car.

One day I accompanied Keith to a studio for an interview of his. While I was walking around waiting for him I was stopped and asked by a producer and a director if I would be interested in a movie called *Return to Paradise*, opposite Gary Cooper. (Cooper was an American film actor known for his natural, authentic, and understated acting style and screen performances. His career spanned thirty-six years, from 1925 to 1961, and included leading roles in eighty-four feature films.) I was eighteen and terrified and said that I wasn't ready. Whether I would have gotten the role or not wasn't the question, but my fear was real.

One evening in a restaurant while Keith and I were dining, one of the top film agents, a Brit who was employed by Famous Artists and who represented Marilyn Monroe (Marilyn Monroe was an American actress, model, and singer. Famous for playing comic "blonde bombshell" characters, she became one of the most popular sex symbols of the 1950s and was emblematic of the era's attitudes towards sexuality), Elizabeth Taylor (Dame Elizabeth Rosemond Taylor, DBE was a British-born American actress, businesswoman, and humanitarian) began her career as a child actress in the early 1940s, and was one of the most popular stars of classical Hollywood cinema in the 1950s) , and many others, came to our table and asked me to sign with his agency, which I did. A few days later I was immediately cast in a tiny part in a movie called *The Racers*, starring Kirk Douglas (he is an American actor, producer, director, and author. He is one of the last surviving stars of the film industry's Golden Age.) I was brought to the wardrobe lady who told me that I would be wearing a dress that was worn by Marilyn Monroe.

This round, figure-less, hefty, elderly lady with breasts hanging to her waist, told me in a thick Russian accent, "Darlink, you should have breasts like mine."

This was my first experience as an adult at the studios, so I kept very still; I didn't even laugh.

At the age of eighteen, I did not drive and asked for a ride home after work. I was informed that Mr. Douglas was going my way and would give me a lift. I was told to go to his dressing room, which I did. He talked to me for a minute.

"You may not be the most beautiful girl I've ever seen, but you have something," Douglas said and then grabbed me.

"But aren't you married? You married a Belgian woman, no?" I asked.

"Now you're acting like a typical American," Douglas replied.

"Excuse me," I said, "but I'll find another ride."

"No please," Douglas said pleadingly, "let me drive you."

I decided not to embarrass him, realizing others were watching the door, and accepted the ride.

Douglas, while driving, said, "Diane, I'm sorry you misinterpreted my intentions, I meant you no offense."

"Why are you pretending you tried nothing?" I asked. "I may have been naive to come to your dressing room, but don't treat me as if I'm crazy."

"What are you? A professional virgin?"

I got out of the car on Fairfax and Santa Monica Boulevard, which made him wonder where I was going from there.

Agent Hugh French's invitation to his house in Malibu to get to know me better had to be handled, so I simply told him I was in love. There was a story circulating at Famous Artists about Hugh French (he was born on January 30, 1910 in London, England. He was an actor and producer, known for "*A Woman's Vengeance* (1948), *Fancy Pants* (1950), and *Under Milk Wood* (1972) he gave up acting in the 1950s to become a top agent for the Hollywood's stars). Hugh French had been living with a certain lady for eight years, when their relationship ended and she was given the job of receptionist at Famous Artists.

When Mr. French would come to the reception desk, he would loudly announce to his former lover, "Hugh French heah!"

The other men in their frequent drinking bouts would laugh uproariously. What a fool! Unaware of what was being said about them behind their backs. I realized I would be dealing with a lot of male egos.

I would have to be diplomatic but firm, one ego at a time, I thought, and then my own as well.

I was cast in *The Purple Mask* at Universal Studios in Hollywood, California. The part had already been cast with Debra Paget's sister, Lisa Gaye (Leslie Gaye Griffin, better known as Lisa Gaye, was an American actress, singer, and dancer), who was under contract with Universal. Lisa and I knew each other from Hollywood Professional School (HPS).

Lisa said at first she was angry at being replaced, but then she said, "Oh it's you, I'm glad."

Lisa was very gracious. In the movie, Tony Curtis (he was an American film actor whose career spanned six decades but who was mostly popular in the 1950s and early 1960s. He acted in more than 100 films in roles covering a wide range of genres, from light comedy to serious drama) was cast as a French aristocrat. Ignoring his Brooklyn accent, I thought it was funny. Curtis was very kind; in one scene, Tony kissed me and his purple mask color came out all over my face. People looking from afar thought I was a younger Yvonne De Carlo (she was a Canadian-American actress, dancer, and singer. A brunette with blue-gray eyes, she became an internationally famous Hollywood film star in the 1940s and 1950s, made several recordings, and later acted on television and stage.) There was a definite similarity in looks between Yvonne De Carlo and me.

I had an appointment with Harry Cohn (he was the co-founder, president, and production director of Columbia Pictures Corporation and the head of Columbia at the time). He told me that he could make me a big star, that I would enjoy a wonderful life and be wealthy, then rattled off a list of well-known stars he had placed on the screen, all the clichés that often bore results for Harry, but not necessarily for the girls.

He then proceeded to place his hand on my breast.

I literally walked out backwards saying, "No thank you."

"You don't know what you're missing!" He yelled down the hall at me.

A pair of French Russian friends, the Appels, who were close friends of Papa and Maman, were also the official Hollywood reporters for the well-known French photo magazine (Photo is a French magazine about photography previously published by Hachette Filipacchi Médias, and currently owned by EPMA). The Appel house was often filled with celebrities, among them Jean and Malou Belon, who owned a very popular restaurant at the time, The Villa Frascati, at the corner of Laurel and Sunset Boulevard, across the street from Schwab's Drugstore. The Belons took an immediate interest in me and offered to become my personal managers. They had introduced Denise Darcel (was a sultry French actress in Hollywood films of the postwar years who was known for her great beauty, heavy Gallic accent and her voluptuous figure and singer). The Belons had represented Denise Darcel to Hollywood and felt I had a better chance. I thought, why not? I knew you needed connections and they had many. They took me to a glittering party at the Beverly Wilshire hotel, one of the big names in attendance was Huntington Hartford, who spotted me and never left my side the whole time. (George Huntington Hartford II was an American businessman, philanthropist, stage and film producer, and art collector. He was also heir to the A&P supermarket fortune). The Belons informed him that as my personal managers, they would decide with whom I was allowed to associate. Although only eighteen, I informed the Belons that I was not a child and did not want my personal life managed, so I withdrew from that association, but we remained on good terms.

The Belons, undaunted, invited me to their home. I had received gifts and flowers from Jean Belon and was explained that Jean, who was extremely attractive by the way, had taken a personal liking to me.

Malou explained, "Give a man his freedom and he'll always return to you."

Malou told me that when I grew older and wiser, I would understand all of this. How very French, I thought. I could never be unfaithful to Keith. Little did I know! I told Maman about the Belons and Maman laughed.

As an example of Keith's generosity and devotion to the Irish clan was Keith's friendship with Dan O'Herlihy, a talented actor. When Keith was given a part in a picture instead of Danny, he said, "I don't understand why they gave you the part—I'm a better actor and I'm also better looking."

Keith laughed and agreed. Danny's career had yet to be established; Danny was a struggling actor with five children. Keith, being an inveterate gadabout, devoted little time to rehearsing, training, reading scripts, and pursuing casting calls, unlike most serious actors. Danny was cast in director-Luis Bunuel's *Robinson Crusoe*. It was a small independent movie. Keith as well as many others thought Danny gave a touching performance. Keith had an idea. He thought maybe Danny might have a chance at the Oscars.

One night Keith and I were at dinner at the O'Herlihy house. Keith suggested to Danny that he would contact as many people in the Screen Actors Guild (SAG) and ask them to vote for Danny. At that time everyone with a SAG card was able to vote and so many members never bothered to vote.

Danny said to Keith, "If you do this for me, I'll make sure you're in every one of my pictures."

Keith had many, many friends and asked his friends to tell their friends to vote for Danny, a real get out vote campaign. Danny ended up being one of the five nominees and this out of a small independent production. Needless to say, the big studios were not happy. As with everything else in life, it was to do with money, and the following year the voting system was changed.

Danny invited Keith and me to the awards, and Keith asked Danny "Are you happy?"

"Now I want to win," Danny answered.

Danny did not win; that was the year that Marlon Brando won for *On the Waterfront.* Danny's career took a leap and he never stopped working. Keith and I gave Danny and his wife Elsie a party in Keith's small apartment. I prepared Filet of Cheval Aux Champignons (horse meat with mushrooms). I got it at Victor's pet shop; you couldn't get it anywhere else. In France they would have been delighted - no one ever knew.

Danny was a good person, a devoted father, a good husband, but something happens when one is in such a fiercely competitive business.

Keith was never offered an interview or appeared in any of Danny's many films. I was cast in *The Girl in the Red Velvet Swing*, starring Joan Collins (known as Dame Joan Henrietta Collins, DBE is an English actress, author and columnist. Born in London, Collins grew up during the Second World War). They gave me the role of the first "Flora Dora" girl to get married. Once again they had already cast Leslie Parish in the role as she was under contract (she is an American actress who worked under her birth name, Marjorie Hellen, until she changed it in 1959. She is also an activist, an environmentalist, a writer, and a producer). In the end it didn't matter as they cut the part because the picture was too long. Finally, I thought I hit the jackpot when I was cast in a starring role in a pilot called *Roommates* for Four Star Theater.

Four prominent actors ran the company. Charles Boyer was in charge (he was a French actor who appeared in more than 80 films between 1920 and 1976. After receiving an education in drama, Boyer started on the stage, but he found his success in American films during the 1930s).

Boyer looked at me and said, "You know you look a little Chinese."

I looked at him, at his balding head, his now slanting eyes, and said, "You do too."

As shy as I was about acting, I had no problem saying what I thought.

The movie's plot was about a typical co-ed looking for a roommate; the girl and her mother would select a girl with a very high IQ, assuming that the girl would be a nerd, but instead the girl turn out to be a seductive vamp. The premise was solid, but the production suffered from financial problems, so the pilot was not developed into a series. However, the pilot was seen in Honolulu where my parents had moved. Maman had seen me speaking in French to my "TV mother." Maman called Papa to have him look and he dismissed the show as nonsense; it probably reminded him of his very errant sister. Papa sometimes fell short of feeling sensitive to other people's needs. His estimation was, it was superficial and unimportant; very old world and European. This came from a man who watched wrestling on TV.

I was up for a part in NBC's *Matinee Theater*. It was live TV and had all the disadvantages of being on the stage, except it was filmed. My inner terror made me pray I wouldn't get the part. The director was a man I had met on a previous set. I tried to talk him out of using me, but he insisted, and I performed well enough to be cast in another live TV production.

At that time Dan O'Herlihy, along with Charles Davis, a very clever Irish actor who appeared in over 1000 performances on Broadway as the leprechaun in *Finnegan's Rainbow,* started an acting school in the 1950s and 60s, he co-owned the Hollywood School of Drama and The Hollywood Repertory Theater with actor Dan O'Herlihy. Both Dan and Keith thought it would help me. I was working at the time and didn't take it seriously. I wanted to be a movie star, not a hard working actress who worked at her skill. Meanwhile Keith had a script written by a writer friend. It was to be done in 3D, which was exciting to many people.

Keith had investors who secured their money through oil investing, these people, who liked him personally for his charm, genuine warmth, and wit. He had a way with words and when Charlie Davis, who was also looking for backing for one of his scripts, (everyone in Hollywood has a script) told Keith about it. Keith immediately suggested he would introduce his oil financial people to Charlie. Keith always thought big — two is better than one — apart from wanting to be genuinely helpful. Charlie immediately talked to the investors who had very deep financial pockets, saying his script was superior and that they didn't need Keith. The investors felt that Keith really didn't know what he was doing if he had such an underhanded associate, and they pulled out; a fair assumption. They repeated the conversation to Keith, who was devastated, but said to me that he couldn't blame them. The movie business is like politics; it gets pretty ugly.

Meanwhile, on the home front, I recall Laurence Tierney (Larry), who portrayed the gangster Dillinger to perfection in a 1945 film. In real life he was one of the most notorious drunken brawlers, a good friend of Keith's, of course. Larry and I were waiting for Keith.

Larry had coffee and I was sipping a malt when Larry said in an agitated state, "Oh my God, how can you drink all that cholesterol?"

Then there was another red-haired Irish Larry, who went shopping with his multi-pocketed rain coat, filled with items. One time he felt he was being tailed, so he hid them behind a bush. When he thought he was safe he went to retrieve them, but they were gone. He came to Keith's apartment, explaining he had been robbed of his loot.

On another occasion, Larry exited a department store carrying a small sofa above his head, and no one stopped him. I thought that this was an Irish sense of humor, and my darling Keith was no different in his reactions; anything for amusement and a good laugh.

Then yet there was another Larry, Larry Kent, a silent screen actor who was snoozing on a pile of dirty clothes in a Chinese laundry in San Francisco. I learned of Keith's infinite patience with drunks whom others would have avoided. He brought Larry to Los Angeles where he let him stay with him, giving him small amounts of wine so he wouldn't go into shock. He finally brought him to the hospital. Larry did a complete turnaround and ended up selling yachts to his rich friends in Newport Beach.

Keith had many boozy, and other, friends in the Hollywood Irish colony, which I found to be quite warm, less pretentious than the Brits of that era, and usually amusing, but sometimes their sarcasm, cruel wit, and extreme behavior caused by the heavy drinking was too much for me. One night Keith entertained so many friends who plunked down in Keith's small apartment to sober up that he found no room for himself and checked into a neighborhood hotel.

Meanwhile, on the home front, Papa attended a philatelic and numismatic convention (stamps and coins), in Honolulu, fell in love with Hawaii and decided to move to the islands. Maman was not consulted (so much for her feminist inclinations), but accepted the decision. My younger brother Jean Jacques, who had worked with Papa on occasion and had a remarkable talent for business, yet which he hated, wanted to be a doctor. He was asked to keep the business in Hollywood open for a while. He did, because one did not go against

Papa. Papa was leaving behind some of his famous clientele, with the hope that they would continue their patronage with Jean Jacques, among them Bela Lugosi (Béla Ferenc Dezső Blaskó, better known as Bela Lugosi, was a Hungarian-American actor famous for portraying Count Dracula in the 1931 film and for his roles in various other horror films), producer Arthur Freed (Two of his films won the Academy Award for Best Picture: *An American in Paris* and *Gigi*. On that same night, Freed received an Honorary Oscar, and his version of *Show Boat* was also up for two Oscars that same year, though it lost both to *Singin' in the Rain* (1952), now his most highly regarded film, won no Oscars. He was inducted into the Songwriters Hall of Fame in 1972, **Hop Along Cassidy** (Hopalong Cassidy or Hop-along Cassidy is believed to be a fictional cowboy hero created in 1904 by the author Clarence E. Mulford, who wrote a series of popular short stories and many novels based on the character, played by the actor William Boyd), renowned metaphysical philosopher **Manly Hall** (Manly Palmer Hall was a Canadian-born author, lecturer, astrologer and mystic. He is best known for his 1928 work The Secret Teachings of All Ages), composer **David Rose** (an American songwriter, composer, arranger, pianist, and orchestra leader. His most famous compositions were *The Stripper, Holiday for Strings*, and *Calypso Melody,*) and a score of others.

Jean Jacques was given a small house in Laurel Canyon, where he was to live with me. Our parents had wanted me to come to Hawaii, hoping to get me away from Keith, but I was eighteen and said I wanted to be with Keith. George, my oldest brother, who, feeling very patriotic at the time had joined the Air Force six months short of receiving a master's degree, managed to get married to a student at Harvard. Our parents invited them to go to Hawaii for their honeymoon. My family pleaded once again for me to join them.

It was Keith who told me, "Go visit your family, it will do you good."

Keith was probably happy to be free for a while of a clinging teenager, since I was more at his apartment than my house. Keith had a way to convince anyone who listened, and so off I went on my Hawaiian adventure.

My husband Keith McConnell in Tahiti while filming MGM's 1964 production of Mutiny on the Bounty

Publicity shot for pilot show called Roommates.

Publicity shot for Roomates *with Maureen O'Sullivan (center)*

Victor Rosseau (Marcel Dalio) leader of the French community in the California gold fields and his daughter, Monique (Diane Dubois) warn Lt, Bradshaw (Dallas Mitchell) that the French will fight rather than pay the foreign miner's tax. The true story of this rebellion is told in the Death Valley Days *drama, "The Battle of Mokelumne Hill."*

Publicity shot of myself with Roc Taylor for an episode of the 1960 tv show, Zane Grey Theatre

Chapter 6

Hawaii

George, his wife and I, after a pre-jet twelve-hour flight from Los Angeles, arrived at Honolulu airport and were greeted with a multitude of leis and strumming ukuleles. The tropical climate was a little overwhelming but magical with its plumeria flower scents. Hawaii was not a state yet, but Hawaii's importance was that it was the key military base in the U.S. defense system in the Pacific. There were *haoles* (white people) Hawaiians, Japanese, Chinese, Filipinos, Portuguese, Samoans, mixed races, and practically no blacks.

Hawaii in the 50's and 60's was like the sound stage of a Hollywood film; a continuous beautiful set with gorgeous beaches and incredible foliage. One could meet people you would never have much of a chance to meet elsewhere. It was like a brightly colored fantasy. Most of the people were kind and carefree, not too interested in global problems.

My parents had purchased three small houses on a fairly small lot, on the Ala Wai Canal, parallel to Kalakawa Avenue in Waikiki. This was their first purchase. They lived in the two connecting houses and rented out the third one. Because the Moana Hotel in Waikiki was so central, along with the Royal Hawaiian, in catering to international customers, Papa decided to open his stamp and coin business in the Moana Hotel. He made a very good choice. Another good choice was to join the famous Outrigger Canoe Club, founded by Duke Kahanomoku (Duke Paoa Kahinu Mokoe Hulikohola Kahanamoku was a Native Hawaiian competition swimmer who popularized the ancient Hawaiian sport of surfing), which was a sports club located almost next door to the Hotel Moana, and as Papa always spent time at the beach for a break, he found the restrooms more convenient. A funny reason to join, but it turned out to be a treasure.

People from all over the world came there, some of Papa's customers were Doris Duke, who lived in Hawaii. (Doris was an American heiress, socialite, horticulturalist, art collector, and philanthropist. The daughter of a wealthy tobacco tycoon, Duke was able to fund a life of global travel and wide-ranging interests), **Barbara Hutton** (Barbara Woolworth Hutton, was an American debutante, socialite, heiress and philanthropist. She was dubbed the "Poor Little Rich Girl," first when she was given a lavish and expensive debutante ball in 1930, amid the Great Depression), **then there was Red Skelton** (Richard "Red" Skelton was an American comedy entertainer. He was best known for his national radio and television acts between 1937 and 1971, and as host of the television program *The Red Skelton Show*), **and many other** entertainers.

Waikiki was a charming area right at the ocean, the Hotel Moana and the Royal Hawaiian were the largest hotels with smaller ones and many shops nearby. Across the street from the Hotel Moana was the International Market Place with a series of boutiques and The Beachcomber Restaurant, with its private tree house. Waikiki in those years was cozy and slightly on the honkytonk side - the shows in the hotels had Hula girls dancing in shredded paper skirts with plastic ukuleles. I actually loved the kind of corny yet unpretentious atmosphere.

Papa knew all the shopkeepers and they knew him. Pauline Lake designed in the 1950's and had a very expensive clothing shop in the Royal Hawaiian, which at the time was considered to be *the* hotel. Pauline became one of Maman's closest friends. When one of the moneyed guests of the hotel would wander into her shop and pick a dress, Pauline often would grab a garment saying she couldn't sell that particular dress because she didn't realize it was in the store, claiming it was one of a kind from a sacred temple in Tibet and the design was customized to fit the karmic personality for whom it was intended. She then hugged it to her body and finally relinquished it at the customer's insistence. She did this repeatedly with slightly different stories. Maman and I had to suppress our laughter. Pauline made a small fortune.

Pauline had a son, Stanley Miller, who lived between Honolulu and Paris. He made his fortune dealing in commodities. He loved Hawaii, but the stock market in Hawaii had horrendous hours. He said he had to at least have decent food and regular sleep for six months of the year. Because of his wealth and his mother's, he was considered a very eligible bachelor.

Stanley came to town, and the whole Du Bois family was immediately invited to Pauline and Stanley's house. To add to the romantic Polynesian, European, and American mélange that was Stanley, he had constructed an authentic looking Tahitian hut on the beach in Kahala with a stone-built swimming pool, which was replenished continuously by seawater. The house itself had no closets to keep it authentic. In the middle of the living room hung a magnificent crystal chandelier. Dinner was served by a Japanese lady; the food was magnificent, the wine superb (Stanley did a lot of the cooking). After dinner, sitting in the living room, overlooking the ocean, Pauline, in a long exotic frock, with her long white-haired ponytail, would jump up with a slipper in hand and run across the room after a rat. I loved the lack of pretension.

Stanley spoke French fluently and adored Papa and Mama. He also liked me instantly. He took me and my family everywhere; he took me to all the best restaurants in Hawaii. There was a twenty-year difference between us but it didn't bother either one of us; we had a lot in common because of the French and the American influences. We both understood each other and laughed constantly —it was a sort of love affair.

Three weeks after courting me, he opened his safe with a collection of jewels and a proposal of marriage. He had a little boy of six for whom he retained custody, but he did not marry the mother. I was flattered after Keith's reluctance, and to be showered with so much luxury and instant approval, but I told him gently that I loved someone else. I didn't realize at the time that I was turning down one eccentric in favor of another eccentric. I assumed that all these male behaviors were the norm, so it was a question of selecting the one I had bonded with to the greatest degree. Pauline who had repeatedly told her son, "They're all after your money," was surprised when Stanley told her he had been turned down.

Pauline came over to me and asked, "What's the matter with my son?"

Stanley, for his part, thanked me for helping him with his mother's hold on him. He returned to Paris to wed his child's mother, which did not last long. Later, returning to Hawaii, he told me that I was to blame.

After the honeymoon, George and his wife went to Berkeley and I thought of returning to Los Angeles; but I was offered a role in *South Pacific* (1958) motion picture adaptation of the stage musical by Rodgers and Hammerstein, starring **Mitzi Gaynor**, (Mitzi Gaynor is an American actress, singer, and dancer. Notable films included *There's No Business Like Show Business* (1954), which featured Irving Berlin's music, Irving Berlin was an American composer and lyricist, widely considered one of the greatest songwriters in American history. His music forms a great part of the Great American Songbook), **and** Rossano Brazzi (he was an Italian actor). I was cast as one of nineteen nurses. It was being shot in Maui, Hawaii, and the producer had invited me to dinner with the promise of a screen test and a possible contract.

I felt the screen test would be a reward for favors and I said, " No."

Then mysteriously I was told that I had screen credits and was overqualified and none of the other girls had the same credentials. I headed home, I then bumped into Assistant Director of the film, Ben

Kadish, a friend of Keith's whom I had met before and he put me back in the movie.

I shared a room with another girl who was sobbing about a boyfriend who had dumped her, Jerry McDonald.

"Call him," I said, but to no avail; he wasn't interested.

At first Keith was disappointed that I didn't return, but then he told me to stay a while longer. Needless to say, my parents were delighted. Even I liked the freedom.

One day a messenger came to Papa's store to ask if I could have dinner with the Shah of Iran (Mohammad Rezā Šāh, he was the last Shah of Iran from 16 September 1941 until his overthrow by the Iranian Revolution on 11 February 1979), who had arrived recently in Hawaii. Papa told the man to leave immediately. For my part, I understood my father's anger, but secretly wished that I had been able to meet the Shah; it would have been an interesting adventure.

The Aga Khan, (Sir Sultan Muhammed Shah, Aga Khan III) another famous jet setter, had married a tall French show girl who had become his wife, the Begum (this is a female royal and aristocratic title from Central and South Asia). Jean Jacques, who was in Hawaii at the time, was six foot four, handsome and spoke French. He was asked to escort the Begum to official events, demonstrating the unique opportunities that existed in Hawaii in the 1950's. George, who before he left, met Honolulu Harry, a local character who sold jewelry out of his station wagon, gave another example of "Only in Hawaii." Harry told George his favorite story:

Honolulu Harry was on the beach near the Royal Hawaiian when he was spotted by a man enjoying his breakfast on the hotel terrace.

"I say young man, won't you join me for a bite of breakfast?" the man asked.

As an ever-hungry Harry approached, he almost fainted - he had been invited to share a meal with Franklin Delano Roosevelt. Where else but in Hawaii? (Franklin Delano Roosevelt Sr., often referred to by his initials FDR, was an American statesman and political leader who served as the 32nd President of the United States from 1933 until his death in 1945).

On the flight to Hawaii, I had met a local Hawaiian football hero from a local family, also named George, who invited me to his home for a real Hawaiian Luau. I accepted. His family was charming and warm. Maman's friends immediately explained that the luau was fine, but one didn't date a Hawaiian.

I with my usual naiveté asked, "But isn't this Hawaii?"

Another faux pas I made was in front of the Outrigger club. I wore a bikini which, believe it or not, in Hawaii in the 1950's was rare. I was constantly asked to pose with tourists. I seemed to fit the tourist's vision of an island girl. I always declined, as I didn't want a picture of myself in someone's wallet. One day a black Marine from Camp Pendleton asked me and I immediately agreed, because I felt people were too prejudiced in Hawaii. My parents, who didn't mind, thought I could find a less controversial location.

Miss Liberal said, "Absolutely not; it's a matter of principal."

It's very common when you're young to scream about principals instead of harmlessly deflecting the conflict.

The news at the Outrigger club was all abuzz with the impending arrival of Peruvian Playboy Carlos Dogny, (Wealthy gentleman surfer and socialite from Lima, Peru; the founder of Club Waikiki, and often referred to as the father of Peruvian surfing). Eligible women appeared from everywhere to meet this billionaire. I was in front of the Outrigger Club on the beach when this handsome man who looked thirty-five at most (he was fifty I found out later when he introduced himself). We were inseparable the whole time he was there. Señor Dogny offered to set me up in an apartment in Paris. I declined. Apart from not wanting to be set up anywhere, I explained that I was engaged.

"Do you realize what you're turning down?" Carlos Dogny asked me. "I own seventeen banks in Peru." He left and immediately wrote me - "You have won my heart. Tell me what you want."

I thought Dogny was educated, amusing, and witty, but lacking in empathy.

Invitations had poured in while he was in Hawaii, and he exclaimed, "Oh, all those people bore me."

He was spoiled in a way that frightened me. Money and position never mattered to me - he fed my ego, but not my soul.

Meanwhile, my parents had rented the front house to an English journalist, a beautiful blonde with lovely blue eyes. I was seven years younger than her, but I liked this sophisticated girl, who had a very ladylike quality. We struck up a friendship and went out constantly. There was a man, Charles, very wealthy and totally spoiled, who was completely taken with this journalist. He had his entourage of nobility jet setters and leeches, and every night there was a party - champagne and caviar, the best restaurants, etc. The English girl was treated with respect; me too, but always with remarks under their breath. She wanted to be pushed into corners, furtively speaking. I wanted the distance the English girl got.

One day I had a small part in a picture on Maui, Hawaii and I met the actor, Arthur Kennedy (John Arthur Kennedy was an American stage and film actor known for his versatility in supporting film roles and his ability to create "an exceptional honesty and naturalness on stage", especially in original Broadway plays, *Death of a Salesman* for which he won the Tony Award in 1949), who was also a friend of Keith's.

He took me to dinner and believe it or not, said the famous words, "We can make beautiful music together."

It was hard not to laugh.

I immediately told him, "Not with me, but I have a friend."

And when we got back to Oahu (one of the Hawaiian Islands), I introduced him to the English girl. They were both delighted. When Kennedy returned to Los Angeles, he went to see Keith and told him that he had met me, and about the English girl.

Keith asked him if he liked the English girl and he replied, "Oh I have so many of them, you might like her."

Very soon after, Keith came to visit me. I was so happy. I had all these jet setting types for Keith and I knew he'd fit right in; they would adore him. We made a date to meet at Canlis restaurant, the "in" place at the time. Keith, as always, was late and I was in the ladies' room with the English girl.

She asked me breathlessly, "What did Arthur Kennedy have to say about me?"

I had a terrible habit of telling the truth, apart from being young and oh so stupid, so I told her the conversation between the men, thinking that she would just put it past her. The girl gathered up her party and they left, saying she was feeling ill. She moved out of the house shortly after.

When Keith came to the restaurant, I told him what happened.

"I can't believe you told her!"

I felt like telling Keith he should be with a woman, not a child; a remark I had heard from other people, but I didn't. Because I stayed with Keith in his hotel, Papa said I could no longer live with them, hoping it would force my hand. As much as I cared for Keith, I did not want a forced marriage. Keith, as usual, had friends everywhere, one of whom was a famous Hawaiian dancer, Aggie Auld, and her English husband. I moved in with them, much to my parent's dismay. Keith went back to Hollywood, saying he would send for me soon. My hosts were kind, but drank too much, and I decided to find another place.

I met a girl, also looking for a place, so the rent could be shared. Through connections, I heard that the headman at Pabst Blue Ribbon beer was looking to rent a large room in his house. It was perfect, but the girl never showed up. Not to worry.

The man, Bob Francovich, immediately reduced the rent in half, but I said, "I can't do that, it's not fair to you."

"I'll do the cooking, you do the cleaning." He said.

"Done!"

He was a funny, sweet man who reminded me of Walter Matthau (he was an American actor and comedian, best known for his film roles, in particular as Oscar Madison in *The Odd Couple,* based on the play of the same title by playwright Neil Simon, in which he also appeared on Broadway theater).

I was offered to be "Home Show Queen", normally an honorary non-salaried position, but I explained it would take up a lot of my time and I needed a salary, so they agreed to pay me. On another occasion, I was offered a white convertible sports car with my name on the side, and the dealership said I could keep the car. They had it prepared as they could not imagine anyone could refuse. I did not drive and was terrified to learn. I believed my parents' oft-repeated line that I was too "high strung" to drive.

I was also offered to be the weather girl on TV, but because of my poor vision, I was unable to read the "idiot boards," which normally guided the announcers, so that turned out to be a disaster. I landed some commercial spots on Kona TV. One was a bread commercial where I had to explain about the natural ingredients made from tomatoes, preserving the bread. It lasted three minutes. I had previously posed for a newspaper that had me holding a large basket of tomatoes - "Some Tomatoes!" - in a half page ad in the papers, representing a bread, and the Chinese client that owned the bread commercial, felt I had betrayed him.

"How could you do this to me? I pay you fifteen dollars for three minutes each time!"

Then he fired me.

The commercial aired and was followed by a handsome newscaster, Bill Anderson, who later changed his name to Adam West, and became television's first *Batman*.

Another creative TV ad toting a local automotive repair shop had me diving into the open hood of a car with my legs up in the air. The strangest one had me leaning against a lamppost with a cigarette in hand asking for a light. A light appeared out of nowhere and lit my cigarette and I gave my measurements instead of the weather. The whole Asian crew laughed, and I thought, what's funny about that? Honolulu, on the island of Oahu, is the capital of Hawaii and gateway to the U.S. island chain. Advertising on Honolulu in the 1950's was still in its infancy.

I was asked to be "Miss Toy for Tots", which, because it was a charity, I did for nothing; but I needed work, so I answered an ad for a receptionist position for a local architect.

"I can't take shorthand," I said.

"Doesn't matter."

"I can't type."

"Doesn't matter."

So I ended up making the architect's coffee, answering the phone, and greeting people.

One day he took me to Long's Drugstore and said, "Pick out anything you want."

I didn't want anything, but he did, so I left.

The next job I was offered was to go around the island in a gold outfit, selling a genuine U.S. silver dollar plus green redemption stamps for 89 cents. I made the round of Oahu, Hawaii, found few takers among the suspicious locals; many of them biting the coins to test for possible counterfeiting.

I told my boss of the few sales and he said, "Never mind, I have another idea."

He wanted to make a mold of my figure and create a genuine real person doll, somewhat like a Barbie doll, and reduce its size. I was to represent Hawaii all over the world. The very concept boggled my imagination. The man never made a pass and he was impressed with my ability to communicate. He thought I made an ideal person to represent the doll and travel all over the world for him. He would also give me royalties. I had an appointment to make a plaster cast made of my figure; then he would have a miniature made. I went to my appointment only to find the man suffered a fatal heart attack. Death seemed to play an important role in Keith's and my careers.

I was asked to enter the Miss Hawaiian pageant, which I did reluctantly. I did it because I thought it would get me work. I won second place because I was told later that one of the judges hated Maman for outwitting her out of a real-estate purchase.

The judge was heard saying, "I'll see to it that Diane doesn't win."

True or not, it was not a pleasant experience because I felt that beauty contests were embarrassing, whether you win or not.

One day I was contacted by a doctor, a friend of the family, who asked me to return to my family because my father had leukemia and it was just a matter of time before he would pass. I returned. Bob Francovich hated to lose his favorite tenant and another marriage proposal came and went. We remained close friends.

Maman had seen me on stage in a hotel, playing the maracas in a little Mexican band. Sitting with a friend, with tears in her eyes, she did not come backstage. I thought, Oh-My-God, what if that had been my daughter?

Keith, aware of Papa's illness, wanted his intentions known and sent me a two-carat diamond ring, which immediately made Papa jump to the conclusion that it was fake. He was disappointed when it was not. I asked him to keep it in the safe for me.

After all, I thought, "I'm not married."

At this time there was a man who became obsessed with me, and after telling him about Keith, I told him it was better if I didn't see him at all. The man went to Papa to say that he was dying of cancer, that he wanted me to take care of his obligations to his son and that he would be leaving me a magazine that he owned. I realized the man was probably lying and refused. The same man then had Keith followed in LA by a private detective and had a copy of the report sent to me. I was not happy with the report and was going to Los Angeles to see for myself.

My mother said, "That man is chasing you off the island."

Maman was right. He called a couple of days later and said, "I thought you'd be gone."

I said to my mother, "You're right. I'll go when I'm ready."

In Hawaii you meet people who usually you wouldn't have a chance to meet, like the Belgian Count, who had a submarine with an organ, very much like Captain Nemo. He was kind to me and wrote me postcards from different ports of the world. Because I was often photographed in the papers, I was sort of well-known.

One day in a restaurant with my mother, I was having lunch sitting behind a large post, when a group of six men sat down where I could see them, but they couldn't see me. One of the men explained how he had spent the night with me.

Maman immediately said, "Please don't make a scene."

Of course not listening, I got up immediately, went up to the man, and introduced myself, saying, "I don't think I've met you."

There was great deal of laughter.

"There," I said to Maman, "was that so terrible?"

Then there was a time I was invited to a couple's house where the cat of the house kept scratching me and no one made an effort to remove it. Finally I went to the bathroom and on the wall were pictures of me from ceiling to floor. Feeling embarrassed, I said my goodbyes and left. The next day, the man's clothes were thrown from the balcony by his wife.

The man called me and said to Maman, "Do you mind if I call you mother?"

Maman said to him, "Are you crazy?"

I met a French girl named Mimi deNanquette, who was hopelessly in love with none other than Jerry McDonald, the same man my roommate who played a nurse with me in *South Pacific*. Mimi was in tears about him. Mimi asked me to come with her to see Jerry. She was timid to see him alone - another man of thirty-nine, wealthy, owned a fleet of catamarans, and had lots of women vying for his attention.

Mimi, Jerry and I went out for three months, having a very good time. All of a sudden, one night, Mimi accused Jerry of being in love with me and stormed out. The two of us went to Mimi's apartment, where she slammed the door in my face.

I told Jerry about Keith. Jerry didn't react. Jerry and I continued seeing each other and it developed into a serious love affair. After seeing the report on Keith of taking a Mexican film dancer, Rita Covarrubias, to Mexico to find her father, who it turned out was a prominent painter, and reunited them, I thought, typical Keith, loves to help women in distress. They're so grateful. Jerry sent for his mother to meet me. She was a red-haired little Irish woman who liked me immediately.

One night at the movies, an elderly man dropped a quarter on the floor and I was helping him look for it.

"Don't be ridiculous," Jerry said, pulling out a quarter to give to the man.

I realized Keith never would have done that, yet I was very happy with Jerry, who was very uncomplicated and loved me. Jerry was a rich rebel, living in an ugly apartment in Waikiki, a city on the Island of Oahu, and was a bit of a hippie and a heavy drinker. While he was with me, he did not drink and seemed good without it. He did not tell me, but purchased a beautiful condo on the beach, thinking I would be much happier there. He told me that he had written a statement and put it in the bank, that we would be married very soon. I told him no, but he ignored me. I sure wasn't acting like no actually I loved Jerry, but couldn't let go of Keith. Keith, who called and wrote constantly, saying he was sending a close friend to Hawaii, William George, and would I please entertain him. Jerry insisted on going with me to the hotel. We knocked on the door and Keith William George McConnell answered the door. My God, I thought, I *forgot* his middle names.

After the three of us were calm enough to share a meal, the evening ended miserably. Jerry started drinking, got furious and knocked Keith to the ground. I immediately went to Keith. Some of Jerry's employees and friends were shocked at my reactions as they considered me Jerry's woman.

The next day I went to the beach with Keith and I told him I wasn't sure I wanted to marry him. Keith went into the ocean and said he thought about not coming out, but it passed and the soap opera ended when I decided I had more in common with Keith than with Jerry. Keith told me once again to wait a while, but I didn't. I thought enough was enough and I followed shortly thereafter to Los Angeles, California to confront a very bizarre situation.

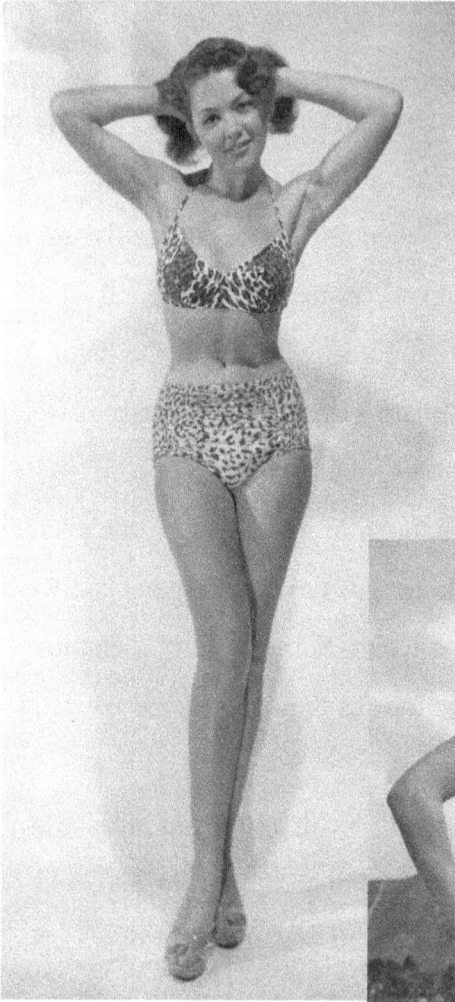

Publicity pictures in Hawaii

Publicity picture in Hawaii with Henry Kaiser, American industrialist,
ship builder and founder of Kaiser hospital

Publicity shot in Hawaii

GEORGE DU BOIS
CANDIDATE FOR
UNITED STATES CONGRESS

Campaign flyer for my brother George
running for congress in Hawaii

PACIFIC
BUILDERS REPORT

COVERING THE WORLD'S LARGEST CONSTRUCTION MARKET AREA

MAY 19
1958

PRICE
$1.25

Another magazine cover done in Hawaii

Chapter 7

Mutiny on the Bounty

Life seems to be a series of mutinies. What Keith hadn't told me was that Rita Covarrubias was seriously ill and had to have brain surgery. He told Rita he had an obligation to marry me and told me he had to take care of Rita and could not abandon her at this critical time, which I really understood. Rita passed away shortly after the operation. I liked the fact that Keith was at Rita's side at the end.

A fellow actor, Patrick O'Moore (an Irish actor born in Dublin, Ireland. He was known for *Conflict* [1945], *Sahara* [1943] and *The Two Mrs. Carrolls* [1947]), told me of another example of Keith's odd behavior. Patrick, who drove Keith to the airport to visit me the first time in Hawaii, because of the restrictions on carry-on luggage, said Keith found a Chinese family of seven. Each one was asked to carry a bag with a present. One was a mink stole (for the Hawaiian climate!). I was so touched by the eccentric but loving ways that it won me back more than ever. I had returned to live with Keith in his forty-dollar apartment in 1959, the year Hawaii became a state. We soon found a worse location, off La Brea Boulevard in Los Angeles, California, for fifty-seven dollars. Even at that time it was considered ridiculously cheap rent. It was located above an iron works facility where at six A.M. the clang of iron rails would rattle the building. Right next door there was a cat and dog hospital with barking and howling at all hours. Keith, in his unique manner, actually asked me if I couldn't have found a place with a lower rent.

At this point Papa was coming to Hollywood, California and I said it was necessary to marry, even though I was up for a film at Twentieth Century Fox Studios located in Century City in the West Los Angeles area. My personal life always was first for me. We took one of Keith's precious cars, but almost predictably, it broke down in the desert and we had to rent a car. We were married in one of those sad little ceremonies at one of those commercial wedding chapels and raced back at break neck speed to Los Angeles to arrive just in time to attend the wedding of one of my childhood friends.

The bridegroom was less then elated at becoming a married man and blurted out, "At least I'm marrying her," directed at Keith.

Keith and I did not tell them that we had just been married because we didn't want the attention taken from the bride and groom since many of our friends were there.

Papa came to visit us at our less than glamorous apartment. I felt badly for my father, but felt this was not forever. Papa wasn't so sure. Movita, who had always remained a friend to Keith (he wouldn't have it any other way) called from Mexico and asked him to come down there to help with an awkward situation - she was pregnant with Marlon Brando's child. Brando said he would marry her, but Movita was Catholic. She wanted an annulment from Jack Doyle, and wanted Keith to go to Ireland to meet Doyle. She felt Keith was the only one who could handle this situation. Marlon Brando liked Keith and said if he would do this for them, he would see that Keith was cast in Brando's upcoming movie, *Mutiny on the Bounty.*

I had accompanied Keith to Mexico, but was left in the car the entire time. He never told the others that I was there. One had to be very young to put up with this treatment, or maybe simple minded or both. Movita was right. Jack Doyle did like Keith, despite everything, and agreed to the annulment partially out of guilt and also his innate good nature. As Brando promised, Keith was cast in *Mutiny on the Bounty.* Keith started out with a fairly decent role, but as time went on, it was diminished to almost nothing, as Keith towered over Marlon Brando with an upper class British accent, but he did have a very long run. I, strange as it seems, was delighted for Keith. Not only would it boost his career, but he was going to a paradise filled with exotic girls, completely to his liking.

Love then took a strange form for me. I wanted him to be free and happy; perhaps because I had always been pursued, I did not feel threatened. I never visited him because I did not want to cause any commotion. Also, Keith never asked me. I also was brought up by a mother who told me that women should do as they like and a man, if he really loved you, would forgive you; but don't accept that behavior from a man! It was so contrary to what most people thought; but I liked to give him some freedom. However, with me it took a strange turn.

When Keith came back from Tahiti, he told me stories about Marlon Brando that were interesting. The film took the better part of two years, partially because of the weather, but mainly it was Brando, who would lock himself in his quarters and refuse to film for days at a time. Brando had little to no respect for the film industry. They, on the other hand, absolutely worshiped him.

Sir Carol Reed, one of the most highly respected directors in the film industry. Sir Carol Reed was an English film director best known for *Odd Man Out, The Fallen Idol* and *The Third Man*. For *Oliver!* he received the Academy Award for Best Director. Sir Carol Reed was let go because of the delays and he still adored Brando. The producers took over and finally got Lewis Milestone to finish the film. Lewis Milestone was a Russian-born American motion picture director. He is known for directing *Two Arabian Knights* and *All Quiet on the Western Front*, both of which received Academy Awards for Best Director.

Brando was always extremely kind to Keith, and Keith was grateful; but some of the cast was not so happy. Yes, they were all making money from the delays, but from a professional point of view, Trevor Howard and Hugh Griffith were much more critical about Brando. Trevor Wallace Howard-Smith, known as Trevor Howard, was an English actor. After varied stage work, he achieved star status with his role in the film *Brief Encounter*, followed by *The Third Man*. This led to many popular appearances on film and TV. Hugh Emrys Griffith was a Welsh film, stage and television actor. He won the Academy Award for Best Supporting Actor for his role in *Ben-Hur* and received an additional Oscar nomination in the same category for his work in *Tom Jones*. Apparently when Brando did appear, it seemed more out of perversity than necessity. It seemed that human beings need to worship.

Metro-Goldwyn-Mayer Studios, MGM, nearly went bankrupt.

Movita and Marlon Brando were able to marry and had a son, Miko, who later became Michael Jackson's bodyguard because he was on the set when Michael Jackson filmed a Pepsi commercial where his hair caught on fire, and Miko put it out.

Another kind of amusing incident: The cast of the *Mutiny on the Bounty* came back to Los Angeles, California in the middle of filming because of the weather, and Hugh Griffith, an Academy Award-winning actor, was put up in a house in Bel Air, which the studio paid for that included a butler. Keith had developed a close friendship with this talented Welsh actor. One night there was a frantic call from Hugh, explaining that he had invited a girl to spend the night with him. When she appeared at the door, the butler answered, took the girl into Hugh's bedroom, and locked the door. When we stopped laughing, Keith took off with a policeman, and the butler and was taken away. I always wonder who Keith called when he was in trouble!

Keith, after finishing *Mutiny on the Bounty*, on his way back stopped over in London, England, where he was invited to a party. As usual he was elegant, telling stories, when he was approached by two men, Albert Broccoli and Harry Saltzman, who asked Keith if he would be interested in a small independent picture. (Albert Romolo Broccoli, nicknamed "Cubby", was an American film producer who made more than 40 motion pictures throughout his career.) Most of the films were made in the United Kingdom and often filmed at Pinewood Studios in England. (Herschel Saltzman, known as Harry Saltzman, was a Canadian theater and film producer, He is best remembered for his role in co-producing the James Bond film series with Albert R. Broccoli.) They thought Keith might be right for *Dr. No,* the first James Bond movie. Keith immediately agreed. There were the usual delays, and Keith, who had not been home in some time, said they could get in touch with him when they were ready and went back to Los Angeles, California.

Timing is everything. Sean Connery, who was a bigger star, appeared on the scene and history was made. Sir Thomas Sean Connery is a retired Scottish actor and producer who has won an Academy Award, two British Academy of Film and Television Arts (BAFTA) Awards and three Golden Globes.

Later Keith and I went to the Directors' Guild in Los Angeles to see *Dr. No* and I, as usual, made my astute observation said, "I don't think you missed much."

Thinking back, I think it was Sean Connery that made that first picture such a big hit.

After the *Mutiny on the Bounty,* Richard Harris became a very close friend of ours. Richard St. John Harris was an Irish actor and singer. He appeared on stage and in many films, appearing as Frank Machin in *This Sporting Life*, for which he was nominated for the Academy Award for Best Actor, *King Arthur* in the 1967 film Camelot and the subsequent 1981 revival of the show. He played an aristocrat captured by Native Americans in *A Man Called Horse* (1970), a gunfighter in Clint Eastwood's Western film *Unforgiven(*1992), Emperor Marcus Aurelius in *Gladiator* (2000), and Albus Dumbledore in the first two Harry Potter films: *Harry Potter and the Philosopher's Stone* (2001) and *Harry Potter and the Chamber of Secrets* (2002). Harris had a number-one hit in Australia and Canada and a top ten hit in the United Kingdom and United States with his 1968 recording of Jimmy Webb's song *MacArthur Park.*

Richard and his beautiful wife, Elizabeth, who were very much in love, came to our house for the very first time saying, "Oh we could never afford this!"

They ended up in a mansion in Bel Air so huge that it made ours pale in comparison. One night we had dinner at their house in a dining room that looked like a tennis court. Richard was complaining that Elizabeth wouldn't help find his cuff-links for him.

"Well," she exclaimed, "I am NOT your servant."

Richard had just been cast in *Camelot*. His career was booming but their happiness was gone. Later, he stayed with us for a few days – different beautiful girls in and out every night.

When Richard left, he sent flowers saying, "Just be happy."

I thought, is this the price of success?

Movita and Jack Doyle in Ireland

Wedding portrait

My husband Keith in makeup for the production of Mutiny on the Bounty

Chapter 8

Regardless Manor

Papa died in 1961 before he was able to see my change in residence. Lucius Foster was a broker who had his own realty company on Sunset Boulevard in Los Angeles, whom Keith had met. He was charming and in some ways highly intelligent. Foster had sold an elegant, approximately five thousand square foot Tudor-style home up the hill from the Chateau Marmont. It was considered at the time a white elephant - in real-estate as in many things, houses fell in and out of fashion.

Some of our friends said, "Why do you want that big old thing?"

Foster had sold the property to a lady that was separated from her husband, a shrewd Lebanese businessman. Lucius had purposely misinformed the buyer that the property included the vacant lot next door. The lady reconciled with her husband. Foster was told he would lose his license for such a scam unless he immediately arranged to get the wife free of the house. Lucius told Keith that if Keith would buy the house, he would move in as a renter to share the payments.

Although we had acquired several houses, we were property poor. When we saw the house, the temptation proved too much. We figured that it was a good deal for all. We moved in, but of course Lucius never did, hoping we would default and that he would take the property over (or whatever he was planning). To be able to survive, we rented out three bedrooms and the attic apartment to tenants. We were struggling, but scraping by.

Keith was quite proficient at buying houses with very little down and became the master of refinancing. Properties continually went up in value. The tenants in the properties we owned were difficult and too often didn't pay.

Keith told me, "This couple has nowhere to go for Christmas."

I told him, "But we can't afford this kind of generosity." It fell on deaf ears.

Returning to Lucius Foster, a man with a brilliant mind devoid of conscience, Keith and I met Lucius when he was separated from his wife Brandy, who was expecting Jodie Foster. (Alicia Christian "Jodie" Foster is an American actress, director, and producer. Foster began her professional career as a child model when she was three years old in 1965, and two years later she moved to acting in a television series.) They had three other children, but Lucius emphatically insisted he was not the father of this one.

"Why would I lie?" Lucius asked.

Apparently he had fathered other children. A relative had left money for the children with Lucius as trustee, which he kept, and in order to obtain child support payments, Brandy explained, he forced intimate relations with her.

At one point Keith and I had made attempts to have the couple reconcile, but to no avail as Brandy explained that her husband was pathological. For instance, he would read a James Bond novel and quote 007 experiences in the book verbatim as his own. Later on he told people that our residence had been stolen from him.

Lucius' secretary, a lovely Mexican girl, asked me if Lucius had said that she'd slept with him.

"Look, it's none of my business," I said.

"I need to know because it's a total lie!" She replied.

"Well, yes, he did," I said, wondering who was lying when the girl spoke again.

"Well you should know what he said about you. He described every inch of your anatomy coming down your winding staircase nude to greet him."

As it usually was with me, I started to laugh and realized men often do this to give themselves value. The girl wasn't so amused and quit her job.

When my first son Kevin was born in 1964, Brandy came knocking at the door and asked me if Lucius was the father. I wasn't laughing this time.

"I don't want to offend you," I told Brandy, "But I wouldn't touch that man."

Brandy said, "I didn't think so. He's really sick."

I told Lucius he's not welcome at the house. Thinking it might be a good match, I had introduced him to a girlfriend of mine, May, who became one of the tenants in our house. She lived in a back bedroom. They both immediately became close. When I heard the news from Brandy, I confronted Lucius and my friend May.

May told me, "There are two sides to every story."

I replied, "No, there's only one side, and his side is a lie."

My longtime friend moved out of the house. Many years later, May and I became friends again. I was very happy that May had found a very nice man and I attended her wedding. Later I came to understand that May still believed that Kevin was Lucius' son. Finally, it occurred to me that it was important for May to believe this, and with this insight it was easy to let it go.

Rather than be angry with Lucius, it seemed that Keith took this lie as more of a compliment. As always, Keith felt a certain compassion for anyone he ever met, which I admired at the time.

In order to survive, Brandy took her children to the studios and had them all working. Jodie stood out and the rest is history. Much later Lucius cried to the scandal magazines that Jody ignored him and finally, at the age of eighty-nine in 2012, Lucius was put in jail for fraud; it was in the papers. There really is no satisfaction in seeing someone you know destroy their life.

Keith and I were ecstatic about our new home. It's as if my obsession with old 1930's movies had become part of our reality. From a hole-in-the-wall apartment on La Brea Avenue, Los Angeles to the Hollywood Hills. The house had a large winding staircase with a fairly large entrance hall with black and white tiles. Classical Tudor houses do not have winding staircases, but straight ones. It was totally pseudo-English Tudor, but it was beautiful with French doors that opened to a garden. All of Keith's Irish sliver looked magnificent. We were able to purchase a lot of the furniture from the previous owners.

The street was Presson Place. Keith named it *Regardless Manor* because of the famous British saying, "Press on, regardless." It was on a small plaque in front of the house. He didn't hate everything English; only their treatment towards the Irish.

I did my best to decorate with whatever monies available, but the real star was Keith. Keith had an elegance and way of creating an atmosphere in a way that few people had. Friends, many stars and people with far more money and fame were really impressed by the house, his cars, and his demeanor. It's really the way one feels about oneself that comes across. Keith put his talent into his life, not into his career.

Edward Mulhare, a very successful Irish actor said, during a visit, "I don't understand — I make much more money than Keith, but I don't live like this." Edward's career spanned five decades. He is best known for his starring roles in two television series, *The Ghost & Mrs. Muir* and *Knight Rider.*

I thought, a lot of people don't know how to live. "Grandiosity is always a cover for despair."

I was as much a part of this as Keith. I understood this much later in life — there was the old ego at work again.

As wiser people know, everything has its price. A director friend who was moving up in his career was living in a very uncomfortable house where nothing worked. It was hard on his family. He had no credit, and Keith convinced him to buy a house and Keith did a double escrow, which was unlawful. He was able to get the house and it was successful. Also Keith, with the help of a professional appraiser, who was a friend, exaggerated the prices of all our properties, which were constantly going up in value. When Keith went to the bank to refinance, they were waiting for him with handcuffs. Walter King, our attorney, passed away, so I could not get the exact details. I was arrested as well. I was taken to Cybil Brandt Institute for Women in Downtown Los Angeles in a filthy bus with a group of desperate, sad women. As I looked through the streaky windows, I thought this can't be happening to me.

I was immediately given a shower along with the other women and put in a cell, calling out through the bars, "There must be some mistake."

I thought to myself how corny I sounded.

The frail, older lady in the cell with me asked what I was in for.

"I really don't know," which was true.

"Honey, if you say that to the other girls here, they'll be nasty."

"You're right. I wrote a bad check."

I was brought to the cafeteria where between the smells and the food, I felt like I had landed in hell. A few miserable hours later, Keith and I were bailed out by a friend. I received apologies from the detectives who arrested me.

"Oh thank you. It doesn't matter."

I was so grateful to be out of there. I guess they had made a deal.

As for Keith, when we went to court, the judge said he had received so many letters commending Keith he was giving Keith probation. I never really knew what happened, nor wanted to. Keith had always paid all bills in time and had such good credit, I thought what if he had exaggerated the value, they were appreciating constantly, where was the harm?

My attorney explained, "And if it stops and you go into bankruptcy, what about your creditors?"

Little did I know that was our future. All in all, I thought the jail episode was interesting, even if it was scary. A lesson learned!?

Our home above the Sunset Strip known as "Regardless Manner"

Los Angeles Times article photo

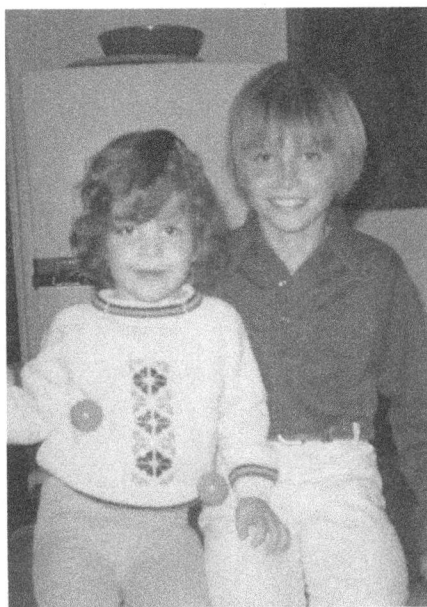
My two sons Breffni and Kevin

My husband with good friend Carroll O'Connor

Trevor Howard with Keith and Victor

My son Kevin McConnell

My second son Breffni and his wife Maribel

Chapter 9

Islands in the Sky

Prior to Kevin's birth, I had taken a trip to visit my mother in Hawaii and brought along Giselle, a very rich spoiled Swiss girl, for company. Let Keith take care of the tenants for a while! Raul Bertrand, the French Consul General of Los Angeles and an old family friend, visiting Hawaii as well, introduced me to a prominent banker's wife who had a home in Tahiti. The wife invited me and my friend as her guests. We were thrilled, Keith was not when I asked him to send my passport, but was not in a strong position to say no since he had spent so much time there without me.

I was delighted at the idea of being able to go and not having to translate constantly as Giselle, being Swiss, spoke French as well. On the plane over an American passenger who was slightly drunk was harassing me. The steward noticed and placed us in First Class, hardly any difference at that time between Coach Class or First Class sections on airplanes. We arrived twelve weary hours later. We were brought into a magnificent Tahitian style house right by the ocean. The comfort and luxury of the house plus the mixture of Polynesian and French cuisine food, fresh fish directly out of the ocean onto the table and marvelous conversations, I felt I was in heaven. I realized how unique this was.

In the 1960's, Tahiti was not comfortable for most tourists - very hot, too humid, inadequate air conditioning - but the natural beauty, simplicity, food, and conversation made up for it. The average tourists did not have the exquisite accommodations that I had. A friend of mine came from Honolulu and my hostess told me to invite my friend for lunch. The girl was a Walter Mitty type, who stretched the truth to its limits and beyond.

As she told her background, one guest, a distinguished French admiral, quietly said in French, "She must have had ten fathers."

The girl didn't speak French, so the guests could have some fun without offending. A similar situation at the Outrigger club in Honolulu would have had polite, bored, and some sincere expressions of interest as she droned on.

A young count from Paris was expected. The moment he arrived, he never left my side. The charming and hospitable hostess told Giselle and me we had to cut short our visit because of some unexpected guests arriving. Of course we understood and moved to a small hotel. Much later I was told the count was the hostess' lover. It turned out to be fortunate because it gave us a chance to experience Tahiti more freely.

I ran into reports about Keith's activities from men that were trying to seduce me. From the local point of view, there was little or no connection between what westerners might view as promiscuity, love, fidelity, sacred marriage, and all those things we hold so dear. Keith and

I had already discussed this. Keith never admitted anything and I asked very little.

We decided we would visit Bora Bora. We went to dinner in a restaurant a few kilometers away from the hotel. Giselle disappeared and I found myself sitting alone. A man offered to drive me back to the hotel. I accepted, thinking sex was so plentiful and so uncomplicated that I was in no danger. On the way the man offered some champagne and caviar (which was not usual in Tahiti) at his house, which was fairly near the hotel. The man asked me to spend the night.

When I refused, he said, "But no one says no in Bora Bora."

I thought the line very poetic, but I said, "I'll walk back to my hotel," having no idea where I was.

He insisted on driving me back and said, "I'll see you tomorrow."

"No, please don't insist."

"Oh but I will," he said and dropped me off at my hotel.

Giselle returned in the morning, telling me, "You really should try a Tahitian, they really are pretty good."

The next day, at the local airport, was the man from the night before that had escorted Giselle and me.

He was the official and said, "I told you so."

Back in Tahiti I met a very attractive half-French, half-Spanish man, a very enterprising type. He had slot machines everywhere, he gambled, smoked cigars, raced cars, everything I didn't like, so naturally I succumbed to what turned out to be a very romantic love affair. He asked Giselle and me to leave our hotel and move into his house, which we did. He lived in a Tahitian hut, comfortable but plain. Gilbert was divorced. He had brought his French wife to Tahiti to make his fortune. Tahitian women threw themselves at men, ignoring the wives, which was hard on the men as well as the women. The temptation was too much to resist, and it led to tremendous discord. Gilbert preferred French women culturally. He told me he thought Tahitians beautiful, but too unpredictable and difficult to deal with. Tahiti was not a good place to be married. His wife left him because of his numerous affairs.

What was once a free and easy island with carefree love making became more complex, as all things in life, especially when things expand. When the French government did nuclear experiments in these islands and brought a lot of civil servants and their bourgeois housewives, many did not survive and returned to France. Then along came Metro-Goldwyn-Mayer Studios, MGM, with *Mutiny on the Bounty* and the whole situation went from bad to worse.

Tahitian women were talking about big houses and swimming pools, things that never mattered before. This was explained to me by several friends I had made. I left Tahiti with anguish in my heart. I had hurt a man that loved me. He thought I would divorce and marry him; I was very sad.

He told me, "How can you do this?"

I had no answer. Privately I thought, you men do this all the time. I wondered how Keith would have handled this. He remained friends with most of the women he had known. Secretly I did not regret the experience. Once back in Hollywood, California, I did not volunteer information, but when asked specific questions, I answered truthfully, also adding what I had heard about Keith and his adventures. Keith was furious but one thing canceled out the other, or so I thought.

Keith decided it was time for me to meet his family in Ireland. Keith's mother had a flare for decorating and once again my picture of Keith was justified. He came from an old elegant Georgian house in Monkstown, considered a posh neighborhood. Monkstown, historically known as Carrickbrennan, is a suburb in south Dublin, located in Dún Laoghaire–Rathdown, Ireland. It is on the coast, between Blackrock and Dún Laoghaire. There was a maid and a man servant. This was my dream.

Keith's father, Billy, who was a sports hero, was also a very good looking man, who had married the town beauty, but was constantly traveling to Europe, where he had mistresses everywhere. The most hurtful one for Rolly (Keith's mother) was a sister-in-law. Small town, terrible gossip, Irish Catholics all. Rolly took an immediate liking to me, because I thought, I'm not Irish. Rolly was a striking red-haired, blue-eyed woman, who caused a commotion everywhere she went.

"Jami's" was *the* restaurant in Dublin. One night the family went there to eat and Rolly insisted on taking her poodle with her.

The doorman said, "Madam, you can't take your dog inside."

"Why not? There are enough of them sitting at the tables."

And in she went. No one stopped her. That was Ireland.

Another time Rolly and I went into a department store.

Rolly tried on a glove and put her finger through it, threw it on the counter and said, "Terrible filth," and walked out.

One day, Rolly was in traffic, driving to Dublin in Ireland and hit the car slightly in front of her. The man got out and tapped on her window, she instructed everyone to look right ahead and ignore him.

Finally she rolled down her window, "Yes?"

"Madam, you banged into my bumper."

"Well," she replied, "isn't that what bumpers are for?"

Yes, she was loopier than mean, but I liked her; the rest of the family tolerated her.

The bedroom Keith and I occupied was very large with high ceilings and a fireplace, also a sink and large feather beds. The maid, Mary, who looked exactly like Popeye's wife, Olive Oyl, only diminutive, about five feet if that, would bring into the room a huge silver tray, which contained a large pot of Irish tea, cups and saucers, two large plates of food, eggs and rashers (like a pork-chop instead of bacon), sausages, fried bread, marmalade, and all the accouterments. The tray was so large for this tiny woman and it was brought up from the third floor to the top floor. Sometimes she would include vitamins and face creams, explaining, "The mistress said you might enjoy these," giving instructions on how to use them, and would walk out of the room backwards.

I thought, all she needs to do now is bow. At night, if at home, the dinner was served at a huge table in the dining room with silver candelabras. It really reminded one of an old Billie Burke movie. (Mary William Ethelbert Appleton "Billie" Burke was an American actress who was famous on Broadway, on radio, early silent film, and subsequently in sound film. She played Glinda in the *Wizard of Oz* released in 1939). Much of the time they were out, but if not, high tea was taken in the library.

Keith's sister, Patricia, lived in a very old uncomfortable castle with her husband. One day as we were being driven by friends, a man who was walking in the rain, his overcoat had safety pins holding it together, was told to join us in the car, and he was introduced as Lord so and so. The Lord invited us for tea in a house that was difficult to describe, papers and magazines almost up to the ceiling, but he was charming and gracious. I adored it all. I laughed most of the time and understood why Keith was so weird.

Dan O'Herlihy and his wife were there visiting in a beautiful house. Danny forever deciding whether he wanted to live in Ireland or Los Angeles. Very often, when one has too many choices, the dissatisfaction appears.

At one point Rolly and I got along so well together, it created a certain suspicion with Keith's sister Patricia, who said, "Oh, she probably wants the family silver."

This shocked me until I realized that many Europeans suffer from that feeling of scarcity, and the whole inheritance business, as the opportunities in Ireland were not as great as in the United States (USA). On the other hand, the literacy and education of Ireland was very high for such an impoverished nation.

One day, lost in the country while driving, Keith and I landed in a ditch. We found at the nearest home, the house was having, what the

Irish call a "wake," a celebration of someone who just died, another good reason to drink heavily.

One slightly inebriated and toothless, but nevertheless kind man had several of the people come out and pull the car out of the ditch. I didn't look Irish and he asked my origin. I told him I was born in Belgium.

"They speak French there don't they?" The man asked and started speaking French.

That doesn't happen too often in America. Keith belonged to the privileged few in Ireland and never adjusted completely to the American ways. A feeling of entitlement is as hard a thing to overcome for the rich as it is for the poor.

Chapter 10

Return to Paradise

I found out I was going to have a child just before going to Ireland but decided not to say anything to the family so as not to have unwanted attention. I wanted to get to know the family without pressure.

Ireland was an amazing experience. Whimsical, like going into the past, this pleased me. We returned to Los Angeles, but at least to a lovely house. I could hardly wait to create a home that I imagined in my dreams. Kevin was born August 1964, a beautiful little boy, blue-eyed and blonde.

Keith and I had rented rooms in the house and an attic apartment as well. Keith was adding to the real-estate collection and as things improved, the tenants left, except for the attic apartment. Kevin was a year and a half old when a friend of ours called from the airport, a French lady called Suzette, whose husband was Irish and an old friend of Keith's. Her husband had died and she had no place to go. As you might expect, Keith immediately picked her up and said she could stay with us. The next day I had a job interview. Suzette said she would look after Kevin. We came back as quickly as possible to find Suzette lying on her bed with a bottle of beer, staring at the ceiling with Kevin nowhere in sight. Frantically, we rushed to the pool where Kevin was perched on the last step in the pool, the water up to his neck.

I called the police, explaining the situation and adding, "If you don't remove this woman, I'll kill her."

They took her away screaming.

I still did not drive. Keith loved entertaining. With the baby, the house work, and this incident, I told Keith, we need a housekeeper.

"We can't afford one, or we'd have to move."

"Well", I said quietly, "then we'll have to move."

We got a housekeeper. As I look back, I never understood the power I had. We hit the jackpot, with nineteen-year-old Norma from Mexico. She was honest, a perfect housekeeper, and cooked beautifully when asked; plus she adored Kevin. Many friends had maids and changed them constantly, not us.

We entertained frequently, and had lovely dinner parties. One night we had all the members of the famous Gate Theater of Dublin over including its founders, Hilton Edwards and Micheal MacLiammoir. Hilton Edwards was an English-born Irish actor, lighting designer and theatrical producer. He was the son of Thomas George Cecil Edwards and Emily Edwards. Alfred Willmore, known as Micheál Mac Liammóir, was a British actor, dramatist, impresario, writer, poet and painter. Mac Liammóir was born to a Protestant family living in the Kensal Green district of London. As usual with the Irish, funny, witty and nasty remarks were passed around. Richard Harris, who was a rising star, was claiming that he was often late on the set.

Michael O'Herlihy, who had become a director at Disney Studios, replied, "Well, you'd never work for me."

Richard replied, "I don't do Disney."

Everyone laughed. Anything for the turn of a phrase.

One felt a kind of atmosphere that was a little rare in Hollywood. A character actor, Patrick Aherne. Patrick de Lacy ("Pat" Aherne was an English film actor. Of Irish descent, he was the son of the architect William de Lacy Aherne, and the elder brother of the actor Brian Aherne." Pat was there for dinner one evening and felt ill, so we put him to bed. Three months later he was still there. I called Brian Aherne, who was his very famous and successful brother. Brian came immediately, but claimed he was not his brother's keeper.

I answered, "We all are, but in this case, you more than I, so please take him home."

I had a series of Tahitian friends, who visited me too often. I finally had to say "NO".

Keith never minded the guests.

Keith was on location on a film, and I was invited by an actor friend, Peter, who took my girlfriend May and I to a party given by the writers of one of Cary Grant's movies, *The Grass is Greener.*

Oh God I thought, that's the one actor I'd love to meet, Cary Grant. It was like a fantasy come true. It was very casual, no introductions. All eyes were on Cary Grant as he talked about women. My friend May sat right next to Cary. She waved to me, gesturing that there was a seat next to her. This was not the way I had envisioned the evening and nodded no. Whenever Cary Grant moved, the whole room moved to where he was standing. That must be unbearable for him, I thought. At one point, I went over to the buffet table, which was deserted. If he wants to talk to me, he'll come over, I thought. Almost immediately he came over; he didn't say anything, neither did I.

At the end of the evening, Cary came over to me and said, "May I take you home?"

"I haven't even met you," I replied.

"I'm Cary Grant."

"I know who you are. I came with someone."

He looked embarrassed. Actually, I realized he was extremely shy.

Cary said awkwardly, "Anyone else need a ride?"

I said, "Yes, my friend May does," and off they went.

Peter asked, "Why didn't you let him drive you home?"

Peter had recently told me that he was in love with me. He brought me to a psychiatrist at his private home where the doctor told me I should divorce Keith, that I would be much happier with Peter.

I answered Peter, "I forgot to bow when Cary Grant left."

May called a few days later and said Grant had sent her a case of champagne.

Life has its twists and turns. Not too long afterwards, May was visiting and I had a job interview and needed a ride to Universal.

After my interview, May said, "You know Cary Grant has an office here, should we see if he's there?"

Well, he was there and we started talking. At this point in my life I was very liberal, and Cary Grant tended to be conservative. We had a very long animated conversation. I was extremely opinionated.

At one point I said, "I must go."

As we were leaving, he said, "You know I like women now."

Later that night I picked up the phone and a voice said, "This is Cary Grant."

"And I'm Aunt Jemima."

"No, no, it's really me," he replied.

I wonder how he had my number. He didn't invite me for lunch or a drink, he really was shy. We talked again very little and hung up. The second time he called, same thing. I knew he was dating Diane Cannon at this time.

The third call was odd, from saying very little, he blurted out, "Don't you ever want to get married?"

Of course I didn't tell him, "I'm married and have a child."

I didn't want to spoil this precious fantasy. I changed the subject. I explained I was off to Europe in a few days, which was true, to visit family.

Cary Grant said, "I'm making a movie in London."

He offered to put me in it and gave me a series of numbers, his private number, his agent's, etc. When I got to London I called the numbers and was told the movie was canceled. I never heard from him again. He married Diane Cannon and they had a child.

I learned later that Cary Grant had taken a series of LSD drugs under the supervision of doctors with Aldous Huxley and his wife. Aldous Leonard Huxley was an English writer, novelist, philosopher, and prominent member of the Huxley family. He graduated from Balliol

College at the University of Oxford with a first-class honors degree in English literature. Cary Grant was unhappy about his homosexuality and it seemed to help him. It's not a solution for everyone, but for him, it seemed to help. His marriage to Diane Cannon didn't last, but later he had a successful marriage, which lasted until his death.

Half of this chapter should been called *Man on a Tight Rope*, because living with Keith was a difficult proposition. Keith's career never really amounted to much. He never concentrated on his career, he was too busy buying properties, entertaining and drinking. He did work, but not enough.

The tenants often didn't pay. Like most people, we had money problems. The tenant in our attic apartment was a talented photographer, Jimmy, with friends in the movie business.

At a very low point in rental collection, Jimmy asked if we would mind if he could use our house to shoot some nude photos. He had several magazines he was covering. He said it paid very well if we agreed. The trouble was, more offers came for more photo or location shoots.

One came from a producer, who was also a tenant, to shoot some scenes for a small budget film; they paid well. The offer was soft porn, which was shot in a bedroom privately. The temptation, because of the money was hard to turn down.

Next came a regular hard core porn movie, also shot in a bedroom. To my surprise, the crew was incredibly professional and clean, but I became slightly depressed, thinking, is this what we have become? My fantasy was crumbling. Keith was not interested in pornography, he was interested in the real thing. I, after the initial curiosity, thought it was repetitious and totally unromantic. I figured there is no right or wrong, it's one's own perception. My personal feeling was sex without affection was not a turn on.

Among the people I met was Bill Margold, who was a very well-known man in the porn industry. (William Margold was an American pornographic film actor and porn film director. Known as Bill Margold, he was a former director of the Free Speech Coalition and was a co-founder of X-Rated Critics Organization and Fans of X-Rated Entertainment). He was an actor and director in adult films. He visited the different universities defending porn as an adult form of entertainment. He was intelligent and literate. He had dinner with us, saying that he never dined with straight people, meaning us. He was co-founder of the PAW foundation, the charity for the welfare of pornography industry performers. His own father was a Supreme Court Justice. He told me that the walls in my house shouldn't be exposed to these films. Such an odd contradiction (as we all are). We agreed and it came to a stop; what a relief.

Keith had some terrible tenants who would not pay and would not leave a new house that had been recently purchased.

Margold said, "I'll take care of them for you."

He told us later he took a rifle up to the property and said, "Get out."

They did. He was a man with many facets to his personality. I would have liked to keep the friendship, but was worried that if I was seen with him, people might think I was a porn actress. Hypocritical, yes; egotistical - absolutely.

Keith lent many of his friends money, and many did not pay back the loans. Such was the case with a friend who died in Europe and owed him a fair amount of money. Somehow Keith had his credit card, which he used signing his friend's name, rationalizing that he had a right. Victor told me that one day he accompanied Keith to a travel agency where Keith attempted to buy a ticket with this card.

The girl behind the counter said, "Sir, there seems to be a problem with this card."

Keith literally jumped over the counter, grabbed the card out of the woman's hand and said, "I won't be doing business with you anymore" and fled.

Victor and I were more amused than condemning. Keith loved the drama. I immediately made excuses for him in my own mind. I felt his many kindnesses outshone his little idiosyncrasies, ignoring the credit card company completely. Keith's credit was perfect. One time he banged on the door of a bank that had just closed its doors. They actually opened it and let him in; he did not want to be late on his payments. He was able to refinance very easily. At the time properties kept on appreciating and that kept the money flowing, but life was always at a frantic pace.

A rather silly episode: One night after a dinner party, only one guest remained, our attorney Walter King. Keith, who was quite drunk that night, lashed out at me verbally and took out his frustrations. I'd had enough of the drinking, and I told Walter I wanted to leave the house. This was a first for me. He immediately took me down to the Sunset Strip, which was just down the hill, and put me in a hotel.

The girl that greeted us asked, "One room?"

"No, two rooms please."

Walter came back three hours later.

"I'm afraid Keith will worry," and took me back where I went into an empty bedroom in the back of the house.

In the morning, Keith remembered what had happened the night before and ran out of the house in his pajamas and robe, and went downtown to the Courthouse, where he knew Walter had a case that morning. Of course, they wouldn't let him in. Walter came outside and explained that I hadn't run off with him, that I was at home. At the time, I thought it was funny, even flattering, never mind last night's insults. What a fool my ego was!

There was a lovely black girl who had worked as a secretary for a tenant of ours, a music producer. She was in-between jobs and was staying with us briefly. One night she had a date with Sydney Poitier. Sir Sidney Poitier, KBE is a Bahamian-American actor, film director, author, and diplomat. In 1964, Poitier became the first Bahamian and first black actor to win an Academy Award for Best Actor, and the Golden Globe Award for Best Actor for his role in *Lilies of the Field.* After he starred in three successful films, all of which dealt with issues involving race and race relations: *To Sir, with Love; In the Heat of the Night;* and *Guess Who's Coming to Dinner.* He was the highest earning actor of 1999.

They had been seeing each other off and on. The next day she had told us excitedly that he had proposed to her. Sidney said he had to clear some personal things and said he would pick her up in two weeks. For two weeks she was in ecstasy. Two weeks turned into a month – nothing. She never heard from him again, even if just to say, hi, sorry for the change of heart. I've often wondered why none of the heroic figures in the scripts that many stars portray seem to touch their own behavior?

It reminded me of another situation when I was hired to hand out Japanese food for a company that was trying to establish itself in the U.S. I was told it was a modeling job. I was simply handing out samples of Japanese food, dressed in a Kimono.

Rosalind Russell, whom I always admired, came up to me, obviously not convinced that I was Japanese. (Catherine Rosalind Russell was an American actress, comedian, screenwriter and singer, known for her role as fast-talking newspaper reporter Hildy Johnson in the Howard Hawks screwball comedy *His Girl Friday* [1940], as well as for her portrayals of Mame Dennis in *Auntie Mame* [1958] and Rose in *Gypsy* [1962]).

Rosalind said, "Why are you working for these people? You know they bombed us at Pearl Harbor."

Russell had received rave reviews for a movie she had done with Alec Guinness, who played a Japanese business man with whom Russell, as an American widow, finally falls in love, despite her many prejudices. The movie was a definite message of tolerance and compassion showing that we're not all that different as you peel off the layers.

Sir Alec Guinness, CH, CBE was an English actor. After an early career on the stage, Guinness was featured in several of the Ealing Comedies (produced by the Ealing Studios), including *The Ladykillers* and *Kind Hearts and Coronets* in which he played nine different characters **Alex Guinness** is also known for his six collaborations with David Lean: Herbert Pocket in "Great Expectations" (1946), Fagin in *Oliver Twist*,(1948), Col. Nicholson in *The Bridge on the River Kwai* (1957, for which he won the Academy Award for Best Actor,) Prince Faisal in *Lawrence of Arabia* (1962,) General Yevgraf Zhivago in *Doctor Zhivago* (1965), and Professor Godbole in *A Passage to India* (1984). He is also known for his portrayal of Obi-Wan Kenoi in George Lucas's original *Star Wars* trilogy.

The war had been over nearly 20 years. I realize how one is stuck with one's own perceptions.

Carroll O'Connor also made me think how we are a series of contradictions when he complained to us that people continuously came up to him telling him that they were so happy that he was a Conservative. The fans thought that the lines he uttered in his TV show, *All in the Family*, was the way he felt, when actually, he was a devoted leftist, except when it came to his personal life, where he was very exacting who his neighbors were. Sometimes I feel we do not understand ourselves.

(John Carroll O'Connor was an American actor, producer, and director whose television career spanned four decades. A lifelong member of the Actors Studio, O'Connor first attracted attention as Major General Colt in the 1970 film *Kelly's Heroes*.)

Chapter 11

Are You Being Served?

My agent, Hugh French, sent me on screen interviews for French girls only. In those days typecasting was prevalent. I decided to visit the agency and as I was walking there, Charles Feldman, who was the head of Famous Artists, was walking out of the building, staring at me in the street and then turned around to look at me. I felt like telling him, I'm already with your agency. Charles K. Feldman was a Hollywood attorney, film producer and talent agent who founded the Famous Artists talent agency. Feldman disdained publicity. Feldman was an enigma to Hollywood. I asked at the desk about other agents in the agency and was told to see Henry Wilson, who had many gay actors, including Rock Hudson (Rock Hudson was an American actor, generally known for his turns as a leading man during the 1950s and 1960s), Tab Hunter (Tab Hunter was an American actor, pop singer, film producer, and author. He has starred in more than 40 films and is a well-known Hollywood star of the 1950s and 1960s, just to mention part of his résumé).

That day his office was filled with young gay men.

Wilson seemed to like me and turned around to the men and said, "She looks sexy but has class. We could make a star of her. What do you think?"

Complete silence. I left, realizing that I had never made the slightest effort towards my career. I didn't like acting school, refused to do plays I was offered out of total fear, and thought I could be a movie star by just walking across the room and charming people with my ability to talk. I had done a few movies and TV shows, nothing much. I realized I was unrealistic and decided to forget acting. It wasn't a hard decision.

Now that I had an excellent housekeeper, I wanted to help financially. I had never had a job, except for acting. Some of my oriental girlfriends told me about a cocktail waitress job at a private key club in downtown Chinatown, the *Club Dynasty*.

"A cocktail waitress?"

"Oh no," my friends assured me it was a very respectable high-end club - doctors, lawyers, judges, and politicians went there.

I thought it's far away from home, no one will know I'm there. The girls also told me they only hire Orientals. I told them I would say I'm half French, half Chinese, Deanne Chan. Much to my friends' surprise, I was hired; I resigned myself. The costume was a black satin strapless top and shorts, with a black and red satin vest and shear black stockings. I thought of it as a movie part. I looked with suspicion at the other girls wondering what their lives were like. The girls were Japanese and the waiters were Chinese. Since the girls all shared tips, when I hesitated to pick up what seemed to be what I thought was a mistake or too large a tip, I got a poke in the ribs.

"Don't be stupid, pick it up."

Nearsighted, hesitant, and embarrassed, I was not up to par with the rest of the girls who were fast and efficient, but one thing I could do was talk to the customers, so, I more than kept the tips high.

The bartender said, "Stop saying thank you every time I make you drinks."

Clearly I was not in my element. The manager would go out of his way to introduce me to his customers. I was terrified I might meet people that I knew.

Sometimes the girls would push me and say, "The customer wants you."

Keith drove me to work and picked me up in a Rolls Royce; no one quite understood what my situation was. I thought, this must be what it's like to be in a harem. One Japanese American girl befriended me and lived near me, so she was able to drive me home. We became friends. The other girls just tolerated me. The Chinese staff seemed to like me more once they knew me.

One night, sometime after his presidency, Richard Nixon, (Richard Milhous Nixon was an American politician who served as the 37th President of the United States, serving from 1969 until 1974, when he resigned from office, the only U.S. president to do so) and his family came to dine, and Mr. Wong, the manager, cornered the Nixon family. He sat in their booth. He imposed himself for their entire meal, probably boring them to tears. Ironic, I thought, Mr. Nixon had done his finest work during his presidency with China, and to end up like this with a boring man showing pictures of the rotary club and mediocre to bad food. I couldn't help laughing. When the staff saw Nixon family off, I was standing there.

Mr. Nixon offered his hand to me and said, "Are they treating you well here?" I was very touched.

Once I was taking a bite of food that someone had sneaked to me, the head waiter pulled me aside into the kitchen and said, "Can't you read sign? Say no employee touch food!"
It was written in Chinese.

As time went, on Club Dynasty wasn't doing well. Chinatown had some really good restaurants and this wasn't it. I was the first to be let go as I was the last one hired.

I finally got contacts for my eyes, which helped, and found a new job in Beverly Hills, owned by a North African, Maison Gerard. I was hired instantly as Gerard spoke to me in French. The food was very good and it was close to home. I worked four nights a week and was quite satisfied.

One evening Gerard told me he would drive me home and told me, "People are talking about us. They say we are lovers."

I said, "You know that isn't true and it never will be."
So eight months after I started, I was let go.

It gave Keith and me time for another child, and Breffni was born March 1971.

Norma always found replacements when she took a vacation. Flora, the new maid, was very happy that Norma took her time, but it was getting a little too long and I called Norma and found out Norma was dying in Mexico with no treatment for her illness.

Keith said, "You can die at our house. You're family, we're coming for you."

Once in Ensenada, Norma asked if she could bring her cousin Letty to help take care of her. Back in Los Angeles, Keith had doctor friends at the county hospital and Norma was diagnosed with a pretty severe case of lupus. Going back and forth to the hospital for treatment, I would often have to take Norma by bus, an all-day affair. Norma started getting better, Letty took over the house. Miraculously, Norma got well enough to resume the housework, thank God for the free healthcare for Norma, the good old USA! Letty asked if she could continue to live with Norma and work for outside people while also helping Norma. What luck!

Now that all was in order, I decided to look for work. A bartender friend told me about Trader Vic's, a popular Polynesian restaurant, connected to the Beverly Hilton in Beverly Hills. The maitre'd, Alex, was a handsome distinguished white Russian, who came from the same part of Russia (Georgia) as my father. He insisted that I dine with him whenever I worked. The food was good, as was the conversation, so I was happy. The other girls quit constantly because of the poor tips (only when serving cocktails were the tips good) and as my job consisted of greeting and seating people, I stayed, hoping it would improve.

Then one evening the maitre'd of L'Escoffier at the Hilton, Leo Waters, came down to get some snacks for himself, saw me and asked if I would be a hostess at L'Escoffier, then considered one the top restaurants of the time. Alex was furious with Leo and me, but finally understood I was making no money.

Off I went to L'Escoffier where the manger gave me an allowance for evening dresses. The manager was a Hungarian; at the time the Hilton had many Hungarians because of Conrad Hilton, he had been married to Zsa Zsa Gabor. Zsa Zsa Gabor was a Hungarian-American actress and socialite. Her sisters were actresses Eva and Magda Gabor. Gabor began her stage career in Vienna and was crowned Miss Hungary in 1936. She emigrated from Hungary to the United States in 1941.

The Hiltons told me to go to Robinson's department store, which was next door. I did, saw the prices and thought this is good for two dresses a year, and some kind patrons suggested that I go to some very nice second-hand shops where very wealthy Beverly Hills matrons sold their dresses. Some still had the price tags, for a quarter of the price, sometimes less. All in all, everyone was pleased with the results.

L'Escoffier itself was on the top floor, with the windows surrounding the restaurant. Four steps down from the restaurant was a dance floor with a few tables for drinks and a full orchestra, reminiscent of old nightclubs, no flashing lights, and breaks between dances. Most important, the food was tip top, all supervised by Leo Waters, the French Canadian maitre'd, who knew his turf and food. He liked me, because I spoke French and understood about food; he had me sampling the food and asked my opinion.

At the beginning I was told to eat at the commissary with the rest of the employees.

I went, looked and tasted the gray soggy spaghetti and told Leo, "I can't eat there, it's uneatable. Why do they give all those workers that kind of food? They do all the hard work, maybe that's all they get to eat."

Leo agreed and said, "Eat with me."

We were served marvelous food from the L'Escoffier kitchen, served by a waiter. I had to stop though because it was deemed unfair by the others, which it was. I ended up eating at the coffee shop, which had food from Mr. H, another restaurant at the Hilton. There were three or four other girls who did the cocktails. For emergencies, I did it.

But Leo said, "I want you at the door, you know how to greet the customers."

Leo would laugh and say that he and I were like a couple of whores at the door. Of course we spoke French and Leo made remarks about the customers and I laughed.

One of the sweeter girls asked, "What did Leo say?" and I translated.

This sweet girl said, "As Thumper (the baby bunny rabbit in the animated Disney movie *Bambi*), said, "If you can't say anything nice, don't say anything at all."

I replied, "Then the French would have to stop talking."

Andy Warhol and his entourage came in one night, including a very tall, handsome blonde, with a nicely tailored, very open shirt. (Andy Warhol was an American artist, director and producer who was a leading figure in the visual art movement known as pop art).

I said, "I'm sorry sir, but you'll have to have a tie."

She replied, "I do?"

Another time it was Halloween and a lady came in wearing a man's tuxedo. I directed her to a Halloween party in the penthouse.

The lady told her husband, "How dare she?"

I thought that the tuxedo looked good and bought myself one. Leo was providing food for a party at the Hilton household and had me as hostess. I wore my tux, and everyone liked it.

I changed dresses every night.

Some very wealthy patrons came to me and said, "I'd love to have your job."

I said, "Oh and I'd love to be home with my family."

L'Escoffier was very easy going with me regarding taking off for vacations. I went to Europe a couple of times and went to Hawaii every year. I guess sometimes one's luck runs out. Keith was on location, and I went to Hawaii to visit my mother. I was invited on a boat to a party by someone I knew for years, but not well. I had no plans, so I accepted. The man was very good looking. I had always found him very cold.

As we sailed into the sunset, he said, "Let's go below."

"Why?"

"Because they want privacy on deck."

"Oh, I see." I was told long ago that I was not very street smart.

Many people think that you can fight a rapist; he was much stronger than I. I appraised the situation very quickly and decided that he must be very disturbed and pretended to be enthusiastic to satisfy his ego. Truthfully, I thought he might throw me overboard. Later, I realized nothing had been going on on deck. I felt foolish and depressed. The next day he called and asked to meet me at the Outrigger Club, which I did. Feeling quite safe with all the people at the beach, I listened to him telling me what the rules would be, and how we were going to see each other.

When he finished, I looked at him intently and said, "Not interested."

In my mind I call it the non-rape.

I went for a swim and was followed by a prominent doctor friend of his, who had been on the boat.

He said, "Well, if you didn't like him, how about me?"

Isn't it wonderful to be so popular!

One evening a beautiful girl came in with a group of Arabs.

The girl came up to me and said, "My friend wants to take you out."

"You're going out with a man that wants to take me out?"

"You could make a lot of money."

"Oh I see, no thanks, I'm married, but why do you do this? You're beautiful; you could have someone's heart."

She just gave me a blank stare.

Another incident, a man with a southern drawl came up with a big wad of money peeling off bills, "How much honey?"

"You haven't enough money."

He started peeling off more bills.

"No, that's not it," I said, "I would do it for nothing if I wanted to."

He left.

On the home front, a girlfriend of mine asked me to join her for lunch at Scandia's, one of my favorite restaurants on the Sunset Strip. My friend was there with two men. One was Miklos Roza, a famous

Hungarian music composer who did many famous soundtracks, including *Ben Hur,* and the other the stepfather of a top politician.

My girlfriend excused herself, saying she had a dental appointment. I thought it odd to be left with these two men whom I had never met, but I understood immediately as the politician's stepfather asked me if I would like to be his mistress as his wife had a bad back. He told me that I would not have to work anymore. He said that I would only be required to see him once or twice a week. He wanted a respectable girl. I told him firmly that I was not for sale.

Miklos Roza immediately said, "There's been a misunderstanding" and offered to take me home, which I accepted.

My girlfriend meant well. Her own story was a tragedy. Her sister had died of starvation in Japan, and she really thought she was helping.

Well, as life would have it, one night who appeared at L'Escoffier giving a large dinner party but the stepfather and his wife.

At one point in the evening he came over with a glass on his head dancing over to me and said, "You don't know what you're missing."

There goes that famous line again. I contained myself from laughing, but I didn't feel like laughing when one of the guests wanted to tip me for his coat.

The wife came charging over and said, "Diane, do not accept any tips from our guests, we'll take care of you," explaining to the guest that her husband knew me quite well, "Doesn't he, darling?", giving me a wink and a knowing look.

I was speechless with fury, went over to Leo explaining what happened, wanting to talk to the wife.

Leo said, "No, no, they're very important clients," but he couldn't help smiling.

The indignity of it!

It reminded one of a funny joke, where a man and his wife were at a Broadway play looking at the lineup of chorus girls.

The man said to his wife, "Do you want to see the boss's mistress?"

"Yes" she replied.

He pointed, and the wife said, "She's pretty."

Then the man said, "Do you want to see mine?"

"Of course," she said. Again he pointed. "Oh," she said, "I like ours better."

The money was good. I was allowed to sell cigars, take care of the coats, and assist Leo. Leo had problems, he was a very controlled alcoholic and a chain smoker. At one point he gave up cigarettes and was impossible.

I said, "Quick! Have a cigarette."

One night he was drunk, which was really unusual for him, and when the Dali Lama and his group came in, he insisted that I put a tie on him. I had to pull Leo away. Finally others came to the rescue. The 14th Dalai Lama is the current Dalai Lama. Dalai Lamas are important monks of the Gelug school, the newest school of Tibetan Buddhism which was formally headed by the Ganden Tripas.

Leo was so talented and ran such a tight ship and with his knowledge of food, that the management looked the other way at his little indiscretions. He also pointed out other wealthy ladies that he had been intimate with. He was an odd fellow and very popular, and I was very fond of him. He treated me with respect, so I thought. One night a dish washer from the kitchen came up to me and offered $50 in cash to go out with him, a Mexican boy who could hardly speak English. I told him gently that I was married. He immediately understood, more than some of the others. I figured the staff had egged him on.

I was constantly asked by tourists what sights to see on Hollywood boulevard. Except for the Grauman's Chinese Theater, which was always tourist ready, I was at a loss as the Hollywood Boulevard I had known as a child had become a very sorry sight. I told them instead to go to the other popular cities in California such as Beverly Hills, Bel Air, Westwood, and Malibu. The request for Hollywood Boulevard was continuous and I started thinking, why not completely redo Hollywood Boulevard from Hollywood and Highland to Hollywood and Vine. I formulated a plan, which would include restoring the old Egyptian Movie Theater to its former glory (the Roosevelt Hotel had already been restored), have top notch theaters with first run plays like Broadway in New York, acting schools, beautiful outside cafes like in Paris and Rome (except in Los Angeles we have the weather for it), exclusive shops like in Beverly Hills, and reopen the Brown Derby restaurant. One must also remove the traffic from that approximately two mile stretch, a glorietta in the middle and little shuttle cars for people who want them. Then I thought of the appropriate name, "The Boulevard." It can't help but be a success! I talked to the Mayor of Hollywood at the time, Johnny Grant, who wasn't too impressed, so many of the stores were closed, the people in the street looked shabby; a lot of pan handling. Hollywood Boulevard was famous for never having been what people imagined.

I told my ideas to Leo, and one night when I arrived at work, Leo said, "Go to the Beverly Wilshire Hotel and present your ideas to this man I know, he's very rich and influential."

Off I went.

"Hello, Leo sent me." I started to explain what I thought was a marvelous idea to this man who looked slightly like a character out of *The Sopranos.*

Smiling and listening quietly to me, he told me that this was not his line of business and wished me good luck and good night. I was not angry but disappointed that Leo had done this to me. Leo apologized, said he realized that he hadn't treated me well.

Leo was a French Canadian but claimed that he was Italian. He had a reverence for the Mafia, which he explained to me solemnly was just another form of government.

"Yes, except they only care about their own, whom they treat ruthlessly," I replied.

One of the Mafia came in the restaurant one night, with a voice box in place on his neck so he could speak and a beautiful girl on his arm. Leo told me with some admiration, that his throat had been injured by a bullet. I noticed that the girl had a beautiful dress, but had a hard time dealing with her knife and fork.

There were other colorful episodes at the restaurant. One evening a tall woman of six foot two came in dressed like Marie Antoinette, wig and all, with two black female attendants carrying her long train, except if you looked at the face, it looked like Boris Karloff in drag. Apparently she was a titled German who visited from time to time. The two attendants were seated at the table, smoking, looking bored; I tried not to stare.

The sommelier, Lupe, a former French policeman from Marseille, said to me, "Do you want to try a $300 wine?" (This was in the 70's.)

"I can't tell the difference after $40," I said.

"You're exactly right; after that, you have to be an expert."

Lupe used to drive me home and for two weeks at a time he was charming, the third week he'd pounce. I would talk to him, he'd apologize and it would start all over again.

The orchestra leader offered to drive me home. He was very polite; I felt safe and was relieved Keith didn't have to pick me up until I heard that the orchestra leader was boasting about his conquest.

Lupe accused me of having an affair with a waiter.

I said, "Yes, of course I am, and with everyone else as well."

Keith happened to call that night and I told him to talk to Lupe, who told Keith, "But she's admitted to having affairs."

That night I decided it was time to learn how to drive.

After taking thirty lessons and spending hours with the instructor, who used to do all his errands with me (he must have been very lonely).

I said, "Don't you think that's enough?"

He agreed and off I went. Heaven help the others on the road! I was so happy when I saw a red light.

Back at the house, I was preparing to go to work. The maids Letty and Norma were gone for a couple of days and the replacement girl had just finished cleaning when the doorbell rang. I rushed to the door and opened it to see who it was. A tall black man had said he'd been next door to see the neighbor, who was a tenant of ours and could he call and leave a message (this was before cell phones). I was used to tenants.

We owned four other houses on the block, so I let him in, when suddenly he said, "This is a stick up."

He was holding a .45, a huge gun. My children were due in from school any minute, and he told me, "Tie up the maid."

"I don't know how to tie up anyone," I said.

I should have tied her loosely. He took some of Keith's ties and tied her himself. While tying her, he laid his gun down on the bed. I stood there watching. How do I use this gun? I thought. Do I have to cock a gun before shooting? What if I miss? He'll kill us all. Let him rob us, the children are coming, I can't take a chance.

Kevin came in first, was tied up, put in another room.

Then Breffni, who was six at the time and had seen a lot of TV and said, "You'll never get away with this."

"Breffni, shut up!" I said frantically.

The robber put everyone in a different room. Fortunately, a child had come to visit earlier and left her plastic jewelry all over my bedroom. When the robber asked for my jewelry, I explained we needed the money and everything was in pawn, which was a habit of Keith's to purchase houses in the past. I waited for what seemed to be an eternity, then untied myself and the others. Keith's silk ties didn't do their job, or did they? We all went to the front door, where a taxi was waiting for the robber. All of a sudden there was helicopter hovering above and the police on the ground; they caught him.

The robber had gone next door, tied up the tenant's secretary, who also freed herself, and then she called the police. The maid had been sexually assaulted. The robber had turned out to be a scriptwriter at Universal and had been in our home before when Keith had introduced him to the black tenant next door. He had become a drug addict. Two weeks after this ordeal, I read in the papers about a break- in, in Beverly Hills. Two masked men had tied up the mother and two young boys, left them on the living room floor and had gone upstairs to rob presumably. They came back down and shot the mother and the boys in the head. It took the police a time to solve the crime. Had I read this before our robbery, I would have grabbed the gun and tried to shoot the robber at any cost.

I talked to the police about this and a detective told me, "You can do all the right things and be wrong or all the wrong things and be right. You were just plain lucky."

Later on, it was discovered that it was a hit on the family, having to do with the Neutrogena Soap Company and partners.

In 1980, my brother, Jean Jacques died at the age of 43 of ALS, amyotrophic lateral sclerosis, it is a progressive neurodegenerative disease, that affects the nerve cells in the brain and the spinal cord weakens muscles and physical function (known as the Lou Gehrig's disease, named after the famous New York Yankee's baseball player who brought attention to the disease in 1939). It made me aware of my own mortality and its limitations. I decided I must be home with my children, so after eight years at L'Escoffier, I left.

Chapter 12

Along Came Breffni

In 1971 I gave birth to a lovely brown-haired, brown-eyed boy I named Breffni, which an Irish friend told me was an old Gaelic name. It turned out to be the name of a place rather than a person, but it didn't matter as Breffni turned out to be more unusual than his name.

In his first year, he never cried, just smiled and Adita, the sister of Maria Montez, came to visit and exclaimed that he should cry and that this is not normal. María África Gracia Vidal, known as The Queen of Technicolor, was a Dominican motion picture actress who gained fame and popularity in the 1940s as an exotic beauty starring in a series of filmed-in-Technicolor costume adventure films.

When Breffni turned one, he still did not cry, but yelled at the top of his voice many hours a day. A long-suffering neighbor called and asked why he made so much noise.

I asked impatiently, "Did you ever have any children?"

The lady replied, "No, but I was one."

I laughed, feeling superior, but soon the superiority turned to worry as I observed that my child was difficult. Kevin, my eldest son, had been an incredible, almost perfect child. I felt I had given birth to an angel. Breffni, on the other hand, was different in a way that was hard to describe.

At approximately three he asked, "Am I here again?"

Telling me he remembered being in my womb.

One day we were in the bath together and he asked, touching my breasts, "Did you give me milk out of those?"

I answered him frankly, "No, I bottle fed you, that's what my doctor suggested."

He looked me in the eyes and said, "Well, how about a drink now?"

Then he asked how he got here and when I tried to explain, he quickly pulled away and said, "Well, I'm glad I got out of there."

His questions and his responses were way beyond his age it seemed to me, but as time went on his personality was ever changing. When I put him in a private nursery school, they called me to take him home. They said he did not respond in a normal way and I should take him to see a psychologist.

Sometimes, if I asked him questions, he would answer something that had nothing to do with the questions asked. He was examined by a slew of doctors who told me to hold him in awkward positions and try to control him, all the while filming the episodes. I asked them for answers, but no one seemed to know. I was then told he would have to be put in special schools where they took care of children like that. Like what?

Once coming back from a session, I was caught in a fierce traffic jam and Breffni, who at this point would not talk to me sensibly, suddenly said, "If that truck over there…" and proceeded to explain what he thought caused the traffic jam in a most articulate manner.

It made me think, what the hell is going on with this child?

In another incident on the street on Sunset Boulevard, down from our house, Breffni started rolling on the ground, screaming totally uncontrollably. I was dragging him; the cars were honking, accusing me of child abuse.

All of a sudden I got an idea and said to Breffni, "I have to go to the bathroom."

Breffni got up, took me by the hand, walked into the nearest shop and said, "My mother has to use the bathroom."

Keith could not understand, nor could he accept the fact that there could be anything wrong with a child of his.

He looked down his long nose and said to me, "You did such an outstanding job with Kevin, what's wrong with this one?"

At this point, I didn't care what Keith thought. He really didn't understand and I went about the business myself of raising Breffni.

Breffni went to a special school for disturbed children. I saw many children with all sorts of problems from retardation to autism to the indescribable. The school required a parent to be there the whole time. The psychiatrist would have a session with Breffni, who would sweep all the papers in front of her to the floor. This happened constantly.

I would ask, "What is the matter? Do you know?"

I was never given an answer. Not wanting to have Breffni removed from the school, I didn't make waves.

One day Breffni went with his father to the great meeting place of unemployed actors, which is what they called the unemployment office. There was Billy Barty, the famous midget. (Billy Barty was an American actor and activist. In adult life, he stood three feet, nine inches, due to cartilage–hair hypoplasia dwarfism, and because of his short stature, he was often cast in movies opposite taller performers for comic effect).

Breffni went up to him, grabbed him by his lapels and pulled him (he was approximately the same size), and said to Barty, "Who do you think you are?"

Barty said in a threatening voice, "Listen kid! Stop that or you'll be sorry."

I had to go to the Board of Education to get further funding.

The head man took Breffni and came back an hour later telling me, "That child is very bright, I don't see anything wrong," but agreed to further schooling because of the reports. "He actually made me laugh, he's very funny." And with that he gave Breffni a pingpong paddle, with a giant hairy fake spider attached to the paddle.

I didn't like spiders, and I said, "No please, not that."

The man said, "I'll just put it in his trouser pocket."

"If you do that, then I'm leaving him with you."

The poor man must have come to the conclusion that the mother was crazier than her son.

In one of the schools there was an unusually tall, elegant black principal of six foot seven.

Breffni looked up at this imposing figure, put his hands on his hips and said, "Why should I listen to anything you have to say?"

It looked a bit like a cartoon.

I took Breffni to the market, telling him not to stuff his pockets.

"Don't worry, I won't take anything this time."

In we went. Breffni spotted an adorable little blonde girl with freckles with a huge all-day lollipop in her hand. He went over, kissed her on the cheek. She gave him a big smile, and very gently he took her lollipop. Later, Breffni decided to look under a lady's skirt. She chased him down the aisle, caught him, sat on him, severely scolding him. I peered down the aisle, pretending I was not with him.

An agent suggested I take him to on screen interview for the remake of *The Little Rascals.*

They were very taken by his comments, but then he started cursing and they said, "No, no, no."

I believed in reincarnation, based on a phrase by Voltaire I had read: "It is not any more extraordinary to be born the second time than it is the first time." The logic of that phrase appealed to me. Also that lifetimes were not particularly linear. I wondered what century Breffni came from.

Breffni was eventually transferred to special education classes for children with learning disabilities, where he didn't seem to get much of an education, except that the teachers, first one, then the others, told me that he was a natural leader and that he was very helpful and kind with the more difficult students.

A friend of mine who did charity work was taking a busload of young troubled children to Disneyland and thought Breffni would enjoy coming along.

Breffni used to tell me, "Let's face it, Mother, I'm retarded."

I tried to explain to him that was not his problem, because if he was, he could not have articulated it.

After the trip he told me, "I see what you mean. I guess I'm not. Those poor kids." and seemed relieved.

I wondered if the series of inoculations that he had at a very young age one on top of another had affected him?

He finally was admitted to Fairfax High School in regular classes. At one point the taxis in Los Angeles were having a fare war and some were offering free rides.

Breffni asked a taxi driver, "Are you free?"

He was told yes, hopped in with a rose in hand for a girl he liked and then he refused to pay the driver, saying, "But you told me it was free?"

"Why did you take a cab instead of the bus?" the driver asked.

"Because I didn't want the rose to wilt."

He had also written some poetry, which the girl told him was too mushy.

This was not his first attempt at love. When he was still in special education classes, he had a crush on the school bus driver. She was a beautiful girl almost six foot tall. She used to kiss Breffni on the cheek every time he came on the bus (he was the only one she did that with, he said). One day, he explained, "I turned my face quickly and her lips landed on mine. I saw rainbows."

The school was having an open house and Breffni invited his bus driver to attend. She said yes and he was ecstatic. She brought her basketball husband of six foot six.

Breffni looked at him and whispered to me, "Oh well, that's that."

He clearly liked women, but I was worried that some gay boys in school thought Breffni perhaps didn't understand himself. In his drama class, he fought constantly with the drama coach and his grades were poor. He probably had severe ADHD, which is attention deficit hyperactivity disorder. ADHD is a complex mental health disorder that can affect your child's success at school as well as their relationships. At that time ADHD was not very well understood.

I figured that I would send him to Hawaii, as they seem to pass everyone; also for his driver's license. I sent him directly to his grandmother who adored him, even though as a child, he was called *The Omen* after the movie of the same name because of his behavior.

In one particular incident at the Outrigger Club he peed on the manager's leg because the man was giving him a hard time. Many people disliked this particular manager and thought Breffni had special powers. Forgiven but not forgotten.

Breffni managed to get his high school diploma. He had grown to six foot three and one day he called home to ask why he had been sent to a school with a bunch of oriental midgets. I decided it was time to get structure in his life and thought the Coast Guard was a good idea. As a little boy he could sit in the water for long periods of time, come out and not rub his eyes. Also when he was very young, he got on the back of a sea turtle and swam back. He was a born fish and this perhaps would be a solution.

My brother, George, went to Hawaii to instruct Breffni so that he could pass the entrance exam. After very grueling and complicated sessions, he was admitted to the Coast Guard; my happiness knew no bounds. I received a call from Breffni about three weeks later from boot camp. He said he couldn't stay there because they were too rude. The Coast Guard let him go happily.

The other children - an adopted daughter and three stepdaughters - were to be part of my life, but that's another story. They made Breffni look like the Pope. Life doesn't ask if you're ready for more pandemonium.

Despite an unusual amount of complications in our household, Breffni as an adult seem to be more intelligent than average and extremely sociable. I came to the conclusion that children are a surprise package. As it's often been said, it's not what you've experienced, but how you react.

Chapter 13
The Affair

Messerschmitt was a name that came back to haunt me. The first time was when we were bombarded by the Messerschmidt planes on our way out of Europe. Eleven years later by my Mother's affair with a member of the Messerschmitt family. Life's little contradictions — Maman fleeing from the Germans only to fall in love with one, and Papa also fleeing from them, only to go to a philatelic convention at this particular time to do business with Germans. He always told us while he didn't like them, they were the most reliable people to do business with, and they were avid stamp collectors.

While Papa was gone, Maman, with friends, went to a very popular restaurant in Hollywood on Sunset Blvd. named *Cafe de Paris*. Many Europeans would go to mingle, hopefully with their own culture and language. There she met Roger Kendall, who claimed to be Swiss. He spoke perfect French, was attractive, educated and captivated by my mother, who was quite lovely. The fact that they both came from privileged backgrounds intensified the situation. As early as I can recall, my mother treated me like a confidant rather than a daughter. I understood this because my father was almost Victorian in his views and attitude. Papa was often mistaken for the famous German actor Paul Henreid, who did Hollywood films in the 40's and 50's. Paul Henreid was an Austrian-born American actor and film director. He is best remembered for two roles: Victor Laszlo in *Casablanca* and Jerry Durrance in *Now, Voyager,* both released in 1942. Papa had many customers who would sit and listen to his storytelling. He spoke several languages, was a great authority on stamps and coins, was honest in his dealings, and had a great deal of charm.

At home it was another story. He was a bit of a tyrant. Maman had feminist leanings. She had been brought up in a very structured and confining atmosphere, with many advantages but no freedoms.

She used to tell me, "Never be a slave to your physical side," and that love was an illusion.

I didn't understand how Roger fit in, as she told me this was a serious love affair and was considering leaving my Father. Maman found out from her close friend, the French Consul Raoul Bertrant, that Roger was a Messerschmitt, which when confronted, he readily admitted. She asked my opinion. I was thirteen and not too worldly. I loved my father, was devastated and quite frightened at the idea of our family being torn apart but told her, we (the children), would not always be there and that she had a right to be happy (what wisdom)!

Rodger had been wounded and had some bullets that could not be removed, so he was in pain much of the time and sometimes was erratic in his behavior. My mother decided she could not leave my father, and told Roger of her decision. He slapped her face so hard, she fell to the ground, helping her realize she made the right decision. Later they became lifelong friends.

As for Roger, he had a rather fascinating story. In 1938, Adolf Hitler bestowed the German National Prize for Art and Science on Wilhelm Messerschmitt for revolutionizing the design of fighter planes. Roger became an officer in the German Army. Later he showed us pictures of himself sitting with Hitler, but for all of this he began to despise what Hitler was doing. There were others who felt the same. He refused to do his duty. He was taken with a large group of people who had offended Hitler to be executed. As these people were marching forward to their doom, Roger walked very slowly, so as not to be noticed, backwards towards his freedom. Later they captured him. Since it had worked the first time, he tried it again, this time successfully, escaping to Switzerland, where he became Roger Kendall.

He decided to go to New York, met an American socialite, had a son, David, left mother and child, came to Los Angeles, met a Finnish refugee, had a daughter, Kaarina, and got custody of the child as the mother turned out to be a total alcoholic.

Keith met Roger several years later. Roger had become a real-estate broker. Keith and I did not know the connection with my mother for a while as my mother was living in Hawaii. Keith liked Roger more than I did. I could not understand his mood swings. Along with the pain pills, he drank because the pills weren't enough. We often took Kaarina out with our children. Keith insisted because he said it was too sad for her. Roger put an ad in the newspaper for a nanny/housekeeper.

Many responded and when asked, "Where do I sleep?"

Roger replied, "Like the gorilla, anywhere you like."

One can imagine that those who accepted that strange offer were not the most sound of mind.

Once again in all his benevolence, Keith told Roger that if he were to die, we would take Kaarina, never consulting with me. At one point Roger decided that he wanted to move to the South of France to live.

In a blur of medication and alcohol, he sold his house for a mere $50,000. At that time, it was worth at least $300,000 or more. He left with his daughter only to return, explaining that he could not stand the constant loud music and the massive amounts of motorcycles. It was not what he remembered.

He called Keith, explaining his desperation with no expectations of help, just to talk to someone. This particular situation touched Keith so profoundly that he couldn't bear the idea of a man losing his home. Keith had been offered a job with a very wealthy broker to buy houses in foreclosure thinking Keith had a good eye for locations and telling Keith they would make a great deal of money. Not because Keith was so pure, he loved bargains, but this was his Achilles heel. He didn't want to make money on that kind of misfortune.

Because Roger was a real-estate broker, it was assumed that he knew what he was doing. The law was not on his side. Keith decided he would go to court with Roger, explaining Roger's history and illness, and miraculously, he was able to get Roger's house back. All he had to do was return the $50,000. At that moment, I adored Keith because I felt I had married a hero.

Roger's crazy behavior continued. One day Kaarina jumped out of her bedroom window and ran all the way to our house, because life with Roger was unbearable. We kept her for a couple of weeks, but had to return her because her father insisted.

When Kaarina's mother came to visit, she was totally drunk.

Her mother had been warned by her doctors, "One more drink and you're a dead woman."

Roger told her to leave and she slipped down on the driveway to her death. Roger, not long after, fell down the same driveway and passed out. Paramedics were called and somehow put a breathing tube down his throat incorrectly. They took responsibility for the mistake. I went to court with Kaarina. The judge met with my lawyer and me in his chambers, explaining that after all Roger was a very sick man and wouldn't have had very long to live. My lawyer didn't argue. I felt we had very little choice and agreed to a paltry sum of which the lawyer would take 40%.

Once back in the courtroom, the judge asked me, "Has anyone in this courtroom forced you or talked to you to influence you about the amount of money to be given?"

I couldn't believe my ears. "Yes, your Honor, you did. I feel the money is very little for a girl losing her father and the attorney is taking too much."

The judge actually laughed and awarded $5,000 more out of the attorney's fee. The attorney who was driving us home did not say a word the whole way back. I was worried about Kaarina as she had witnessed both parents' deaths. I had her examined by a psychiatrist. Apparently she was all right.

We all attended Rogers' funeral where his son David Kendall, who was an attorney in Washington (I was told he was President Clinton's attorney, but I never checked it out), very kindly said that he would take care of Kaarina if she agreed. Kaarina chose to stay with us. Timing is everything in life or perhaps it was her destiny.

Chapter 14
King of the Bs

"What's a Zug?" Shouted Al Capone in the early thirties.

"What's a Zug?" Screamed a headline two years later in *Variety,* the bible of show business. *Variety* is a weekly American entertainment trade magazine and website owned by Penske Media Corporation. It was founded by Sime Silverman in New York in 1905 as a weekly newspaper reporting on theater and vaudeville.

"What's a Zug?" Growled Harry Cohen, czar of Colombia Pictures, nineteen years later. Harry Cohn was the co-founder, president, and production director of Columbia Pictures Corporation (film and television studio).

And Humphrey Bogart, out of the side of his famous mouth, whispered, "What's a Zug!?" (Humphrey DeForest Bogart was an American screen and stage actor. His performances in 1940s film noir movies such as *The Maltese Falcon, Casablanca,* and *The Big Sleep* earned him status as a cultural icon).

Albert Zugsmith was born 1910 in Atlantic City. At the age of 14 he was an Eagle Scout, the highest honor of the Boy Scouts. He had a record of six hundred and seventy-eight rescues as a Ventnor City life guard and captain. He was a newspaper editor and publisher, press agent to Al Capone (Alphonse Gabriel Capone, sometimes known by the nickname "Scarface", was an American gangster and businessman who attained notoriety during the Prohibition era as the co-founder and boss of the Chicago Outfit).

Albert then went into high finance as broker for newspapers, television, and radio stations. He finally landed on the road to Hollywood where he was a producer, writer and/or director who specialized in low-budget exploitation films through the 1950s and 1960s, almost one hundred feature film.

Albert Zugsmith's Academy-Award-winning *Written on the Wind* was nominated for three Academy Awards and made millions for Universal Studios. The film starred Rock Hudson, Lauren Bacall (Lauren Bacall was an American actress known for her distinctive voice and sultry looks. She was named the 20th greatest female star of classic Hollywood cinema by the American Film Institute, and received an Academy Honorary Award from the Academy of Motion Picture Arts and Sciences in 2009, in recognition of her central place in the Golden Age of motion pictures), Robert Stack (Robert Stack was an American actor, sportsman, and television host. In addition to acting in more than 40 feature films, he starred in the ABC-TV television series *The Untouchables*, for which he won the 1960 Emmy Award for Best Actor in a Dramatic Series, and later hosted *Unsolved Mysteries* (1987–2002), and Dorothy Malone (Mary Dorothy Maloney was an American actress. Her film career began in 1943, and in her early years she played small roles, mainly in B-movies), who won an Academy Award for Best Supporting Actress for this film, which cost slightly over two million to make including Universal Studio's overhead.

Albert Zugsmith's production of *Touch of Evil* starring Orson Welles (George Orson Welles was an American actor, director, writer, and producer who worked in theater, radio, and film from 1931 to 1985,) and Charlton Heston (Charlton Heston was an American actor and political activist. As a Hollywood star, he appeared in almost 100 films over the course of 60 years), Marlene Dietrich (Marie Magdalene "Marlene" Dietrich was a German actress and singer who held both German and American citizenship. Throughout her long career, which spanned from the 1910s to the 1980s, she maintained popularity by continually reinventing herself), Dennis Weaver (William Dennis Weaver was an American actor best known for his work in television and films from the early 1950s to not long before his death in 2006), Janet Leigh (Janet Leigh was an American actress, singer, dancer, and author. Raised in Stockton, California by working-class parents, Leigh was discovered at age eighteen by actress Norma Shearer, who helped her secure a contract with Metro-Goldwyn-Mayer), and many others, has received numerous awards and kudos as one of the classics of the motion picture industry.

Another famous film of Albert Zugsmith was, *The Incredible Shrinking Man,* it was hailed at that time by the New York Times as the finest science fiction film ever made. It made millions for Universal

Studios; it cost substantially less than a million to make. Interesting note: hundreds of tarantulas died on the set because of the hot lights.

Next for Albert Zugsmith was an Metro-Goldwyn-Mayer Studios, Inc. (MGM) film *High School Confidential* starring Russ Tamblyn (Russell Irving Tamblyn is an American film and television actor and dancer. Born and raised in Los Angeles, Tamblyn was trained as a gymnast in his youth), **Mamie Van Doren** (Mamie Van Doren is an American actress, model, singer, and sex symbol who is known for being one of the first actresses to recreate the look of Marilyn Monroe), **John Drew Barrymore** (John Drew Barrymore was a film actor and member of the Barrymore family of actors, which included his father, John Barrymore, and his father's siblings, Lionel and Ethel) , **Jan Sterling** (Jan Sterling was an American actress of stage, film and television. Most active in films during the 1950s, Sterling received a Golden Globe Award for Best Supporting Actress for her performance in *The High and the Mighty* (1954), and was nominated for an Academy Award for Best Supporting Actress for the same performance), **and Jackie Coogan.** (John Leslie "Jackie" Coogan was an American actor and comedian who began his movie career as a child actor in silent films. Charlie Chaplin's film classic *The Kid* made him one of the first child stars in film history). The film broke the all-time record at the Fame Loews State Theater on Broadway in New York, and also made millions for MGM Studio despite its comparatively low budget of $517,000.

The motion picture *Fanny Hill* also one of Albert Zugsmith's films, starring Miriam Hopkins (Ellen Miriam Hopkins was an American actress known for her versatility. She first signed with Paramount

Pictures in 1930, working with Ernst Lubitsch who was a German American film director, producer, writer, and actor. His urbane comedies of manners gave him the reputation of being Hollywood's most elegant and sophisticated director; as his prestige grew, his films were promoted as having "the Lubitsch touch". Also staring Joel McCrea (Joel Albert McCrea was an American actor whose career spanned almost five decades and appearances in more than 90 films), among many others), and Leticia Roman (Letícia Román is an Italian film actress), made almost one million dollars net profit, although the cost was a mere $345,000. Finally, Albert Zugsmith film *Invasion USA* cost only $127,000 and made almost one million dollars net profit.

Zug had produced as many as eight features in a year when one a year was considered a triumph. A symbol of freedom in the USA means you can be "King of the B's", of low budget films, without envy or even admiration. He was rarely home and his wife of many years finally divorced him. He was casting the film *Violated* when an actress he knew told Zug that her son had a beautiful Danish girlfriend who would suit his film. He agreed when he met Susanne and immediately cast her. He also cast our eldest son, Kevin, who was eight years old. Susanne was nineteen. For Kevin it was love at first sight. The picture was never released; meanwhile, Susanne, who needed a job, worked for Zug as a secretary, bookkeeper, all around girl Friday. Actually there was very little she couldn't do. She decorated the house he used as an office with an artistic flair. She could do murals, lay tiles, do his taxes, knew how to invest in the stock market, and cook like a gourmet chef when he was entertaining clients. When her visa expired, she had to return to Denmark. Zug found his life so empty without this beautiful miracle worker. He had never been treated this well, so he called her in Denmark and proposed.

For her part, Susanne felt Denmark too small, there was lots of jealousy and she longed to see the world. She found herself in Hollywood, which was not a gentle as Denmark. At first she found it large and freeing, people couldn't care less, and then she found it lonely, which happens to many Europeans.

She was not in love like many Scandinavians, thinking love was overrated, liked California, thought she could pursue her artistic nature and said, "Yes."

She was definitely his intellectual equal if not superior, and so they were married.

Susanne found life with Zug confining. He had found something precious and wanted to keep it close. Unless they were going out, he locked all the doors, summer or winter at 6:00 P.M. She was a gifted cook, but he ate a very restrictive diet, and when they traveled, he was at her side every minute. If she thought Denmark was small this was a whole other dimension in smallness. He was entertaining and did tell stories.

He told Susanne that when Joan Crawford was filming for him, she often slept in her dressing room overnight. (Joan Crawford was an American film and television actress who began her career as a dancer and stage showgirl. In 1999, the American Film Institute ranked Crawford tenth on its list of the greatest female stars of Classic Hollywood Cinema).

One night the man at the gate called Zug at 3:00 a.m. saying there was a girl with a goat.

"Miss Crawford asked for it to be delivered to her room," the guard said. "What do you want me to do?"

Zug answered, "Whatever Miss Crawford wants, Miss Crawford can have."

Zug never knew why, she never said, he never asked.

Zug told Susanne about the time there was a hit on him from some disgruntled investors, having to do with the mob. Zug called Al Capone, who liked him since his press agent days.

"Don't worry, I'll put a stop to it," Capone said. He called back and said, "It's done, call me if you need me again."

In Hollywood one never knows who one's friends are. Then sadly Zug grew less and less interested in his work, maybe because he was so comfortable, perhaps for the first time in his life. Susanne, who was so young and dynamic, was disillusioned with his lack of interest in show business.

She immediately had a child whom she dearly loved, but was not prepared for. Zug was beaming with pride, while Susanne was feeling trapped. Susanne began to fade from being a beautiful flower, looking completely desperate as if the life had been drawn out of her. Zug who was no fool, noticed this as well. He was forty-four years her senior and had suffered a mild stroke. He decided that Susanne should have a physical companion (as if people didn't have emotions). We were decent people, Zug decided, and Kevin, who was now nineteen would be a good choice.

It's as if Zug were casting a part in a film. The last time Susanne had seen Kevin he was fourteen, with acne and a headgear for braces. Zug called us and asked that Kevin read a new script that he had written. For many weeks Kevin came home in the early morning hours. Finally I asked him what was going on, and he told me. Kevin was now a beautiful boy of six foot one, but there was an eleven-year difference. After getting over the initial shock, I realized I had very little power over this situation. Kevin was over eighteen and he was ecstatic.

So all I said was, "Please be careful that she doesn't get pregnant."

"Well mother, that's what I wanted to talk to you about."

Overwhelmed with anger, I grabbed Keith by the hand and went over to Zug's house. Both the Zugsmiths' and our houses were above the Sunset Strip in the Hollywood area. Keith was surprisingly quiet, not as upset as I was. Zug knew all about Keith's mistress, which at that time, I did not know existed.

I told Zug, "It's one thing to get your wife a lover; it's another thing to use our son as a breeder!"

Zug, who had always been fond of me, couldn't understand my fury.

"And you" - I turned to Susanne – "Your husband did this for you because he loves you, but why did you do it?"

Susanne was not one to show her emotions; she was very uncomfortable and said, "It was an accident, and I will take care of it."

I had visions in my head of Kevin looking through a window, watching another man bring up his child. I was furious as Zug asked us to leave.

"Call the police. I won't go until I'm finished." But there was nothing left to say and we left.

Keith and I went to Brazil to visit an opal mine, which we very unwisely invested in, and came back three months later. Kevin took me to lunch where he announced that I was going to be a grandmother. At first I couldn't find the bottom of my anger, but when I looked at Kevin and saw he was suffering, I came to the conclusion that I loved my son more than I hated Susanne. I decided to make peace with Susanne and Zug, who actually felt guilty.

Then a strange thing happened. Susanne said she loved Kevin and was prepared to leave Zug and all the comforts. I thought, at least she has a heart, but Kevin is only twenty, he hasn't finished college; how is he going to support you and the children? Susanne was going to take her little girl and Kevin's little boy with them. She answered they would find a way. They secretly found a house to rent and made all the arrangements, and Susanne went to tell Zug. This was not in the script and he immediately had another stroke.

Susanne solemnly told us, "I cannot leave this man, he has only been kind to me, I have to take care of him."

I slowly started to like Susanne.

Then the unexpected happened - Zug said to Susanne, "Bring Kevin to live here."

A bizarre triangle was formed, but it worked. Kevin was very responsible and more mature than his years. Zug grew very fond of him. They all moved to Agoura Hills, California, which is North West of Los

Angeles by about 35 to 40 miles from Beverly Hills area. Susanne had another child by Kevin. Zug, Susanne and Kevin thought Agoura Hills was safer community for the children and since it was in the Las Virgenes School District of the wealthy, it had a superior school system, most of the parents were very active in the schools and the ratio of student per teacher was much lower then the Los Angeles School District.

Susanne and I talked about the abortion, which she never had. Susanne explained that twice she was at the doctor's office and twice he had emergencies. The third time, while she sat there waiting, she explained that she felt so connected with the baby that she walked out of the office. I loved her for that.

Susanne and Kevin eventually put Zug in the Motion Picture home nearby in Woodland Hills, California, because he required physical and medical help they could not give him. They visited him almost every day until he died.

Susanne was playing the commodities market and was swindled out of $300,000. She went to Washington before the Securities and Exchanges Commission and won a judgment against the brokerage firm, but the firm filed for bankruptcy and she lost everything. By this time I had remarried and my husband Victor and his business partner suggested she take a loan out on her fully paid house and invest in the plastics factory that they were about to acquire, which went bust because of the Lincoln Savings Scandal.

Susanne and Kevin could not sell their mortgaged house because the developer was in a lawsuit for improper grading and land slipping. They had another investment that they had made into the development of patent rights, for a unique heating and cooling system that went completely down the drain and bankrupted them. Susanne auctioned off all her expensive jewelry and furniture. I thought, you can really see the nature of a person when they are in trouble.

Producer/Director Albert Zugsmith (Zug) on the set of his movie "High School Confidential"

Zug on the set of High School Confidential *with Mamie Van Doren*

Zug and his wife Susanne in Atlantic City (Zug's home town)

Susanne's agency photos

Chapter 15

Victor Victorious

Victor was born an only child in Budapest in 1932, where the father was a mid-level railroad official and his mother died when he was six. What he remembers was that she wanted him to become a priest, a concept that made him very uncomfortable. Victor adored his stepmother, who was a very gentle giving soul with no demands. Their home was bombed in one of those endless conflicts - life was very complicated under communism.

By the age of twelve, Victor found a way to steal food from drunken Russian soldiers so that his family and friends would have something to eat. Hungarians seemed to be clever at adapting and manipulating an irrational system, making life more bearable. By the time Victor was fifteen, his resourceful brain led him to falsify papers claiming he was eighteen so that he could be employed in a textile manufacturing factory. He was talented and not too long afterward became a manger. He also joined the communist party, so as to be able to obtain a release for his father, who had been imprisoned because he was against communism. His father had not been given a cot to sleep on, but slept on the cold cement floor. An additional benefit of being a "Red" manager was to be chauffeured from home to plant and back in a state limousine.

Victor saw the fraud in state socialism, the hypocrisy in declaring that everything was for the people, when in reality only a few benefited (somehow, all this sounds familiar). He detested the endless meetings, all talk, but few problems solved, and the few that were, were ignored or violated. The backstabbing fueled by alcoholism was torturous to endure.

Victor later told me, "There's nothing fair or noble about communism. It's not equality come true, but a brutal hopeless nightmare."

At age twenty-three, Victor defiantly secretly married his fiance in a Catholic church, forbidden to party members. The girl was Maria Follet, a niece of the Rothschild family. (The Rothschild family is a wealthy Jewish family descending from Mayer Amschel Rothschild, a court factor to the German Landgraves of Hesse-Kassel in the Free City of Frankfurt, Holy Roman Empire, who established his banking business in the 1760s.)

Maria was a concert pianist with a big future. On one formal musical evening, Victor was seated next to a man, listening to the soloist, a woman singer.

"Listen to that woman sing; she's awful," Victor said to the man.

The man replied, "That's my daughter."

Wishing to quickly defuse what he had just said, Victor whispered, "Well, listen to that pianist, she's even worse."

This time the host said, "That's my wife."

Shocked by the thought that he put his foot twice in his mouth, Victor was quickly relieved of any guilt.

"You're the only person that has ever had to courage to speak the truth."

The two men looked at each other briefly and then broke out in laughter.

Victor overheard from his wife's family members on several occasions that he was a peasant and that he had married above his station; this was routine in all upper-class circles.

"He may be a peasant, but he's clever and resourceful enough to feed us," said one.

The European aristocracy had for the most part, and with few exceptions, unspoken but active sexual lives of all sorts - their best friends' wives, maids, secretaries, etc. By belonging to the "Petite Bourgeoisie," it was quite expected and normal for Victor to be shocked, even though Victor had a very active sexual life all the time he was engaged. He thought again, as a proper member of his class, that these people were degenerate.

Victor, in his thoughts, revolted against this tyrannical regime, which made life in Hungary a living hell. Finally, by the anti-communist upheaval of 1956, Victor had turned into a dedicated freedom fighter. He was also involved with liberating Cardinal Jozsef Mindszenty from Red captivity by smuggling him out of Hungary. József Cardinal Mindszenty [jo:ʒɛf mindsɛnti] was the Prince Primate, Archbishop of

Esztergom, cardinal, and leader of the Catholic Church in Hungary from 2 October 1945 to 18 December 1973.

Victor was exposed. They came after him. He had to flee the country to survive. He had only been married for eight months. His sheltered bride could not face the obstacles of this trip. He told her he would send for her as soon as possible. His secretary, Kristina, who was in love with him (when he married Maria, a broken-hearted Kristina married an actor on the rebound), found out Victor was going alone and she left her new husband to joined Victor for an uncertain future.

Victor guided a group of cold, hungry, frightened, men, women, and children, carrying a baby in his arms, in the black of night, over a large minefield.

"Follow exactly in my footsteps," he told them.

If he set off a mine, a volunteer would have to continue. Awaiting the refugees across the river was a large group of people with blankets, clothes, and shoes, assuming they would be soaking wet after wading through the water. Oddly, the party arrived bone dry.

At dawn, Victor retraced some steps to see if the river had frozen over, he found out that the Moravian River was flowing normally. He asked many people to come up with a rational explanation and was told that they had seen so many incredible events, that nothing surprised them anymore.

To add to this amazing story, many years later a young man knocked on Victor's door, introduced himself, and said, "I was the baby you carried in your arms over the mine field."

Victor arrived at Ellis Island in 1957 to the freedom and opportunity of America. To the free world, being a freedom fighter was admired, but the Red intelligence machine along with some corrupt immigration officials found a way to sabotage their release, lose paperwork, or falsify information about refugees to delay or return them to the communists.

Victor was able to discover that the official that was holding his release had been bribed. He threatened the man and got his release. He ended up in Weirton, West Virginia, with a group dedicated to helping Hungarian freedom fighters settle in the US. Being somewhat cocky, Victor refused to accept a substantial amount of money, believing he could earn his own way. Some people offered him instant employment.

Kristina had no trouble leaving Ellis Island. They reunited and then went to Ohio, where they were welcomed. Victor's parents pleaded with him to divorce Maria so that she could continue with her life but he still hoped that she would join him.

Kristina, when she realized that Victor had no intention of divorcing, left him and said if he changed his mind, he could reach her. Victor was lonelier than ever, yearning for his gentle Maria.

He arrived in Los Angeles, California and began seriously working on his English. He was so impressed with the public libraries and all the facilities available, in contrast to the restricted ones in his own country. He went to the movies in downtown Los Angeles, where he would watch three movies, one after the other, to pick up on the dialogue. He learned to mimic the sounds and it deepened his understanding.

One of those times a young girl sat next to him offering sexual favors.

When he turned her down, she said, "I'll scream rape."

He said, "Go ahead." He wasn't intimidated.

Because he had been a soccer hero in his own country, he was able to get a job at a local college as a coach. As a bonus, they provided him with girls who were told to give him oral sex in the car. At first he thought he was in heaven - it was not so common in Hungary.

He said to one girl, "I don't even know your name."

But after a while, he found it almost depressing. Victor liked women, but this was too impersonal. He had, had many encounters with women, but never like this.

Victor had managed to get an electrical engineering degree from the University of Budapest, but he felt something he never felt before - he felt he had choices and that he could take his time. He went from job to job - substitute teacher, bus driver who picked up pretty nurses and dropped them off at locations not always on the route. As an assistant to a photographer who had access to beautiful models, he was happy for a short time, but it didn't satisfy.

His father called again, explaining that Maria was not allowed to perform on stage or leave the country because she was the wife of a freedom fighter. Victor finally gave her the divorce. Actually it did not change anything for her, she still could not leave the country nor was she allowed to perform.

Then he met Ethel, his second wife, a cultivated and intelligent woman who introduced him to golf and bowling. They went to the races, opera, and played poker. Ethel was related to the famous comedian George Gobel, which allowed them the best seats at many events. George Leslie Goebel was an American humorist, actor, and comedian. He was best known as the star of his own weekly comedy variety television series, *The George Gobel Show*, broadcasting from 1954 to 1959 on NBC, and on CBS from 1959 to 1960.

Victor's father-in-law had a good position in the FBI, which proved to be a Godsend. When agents came to take Victor back to Hungary, where they surely would have killed him, his father-in-law stepped in and was able to put a stop to it.

Ethel wanted children badly, but after three miscarriages, she was discouraged. Victor suggested adoption, which she didn't want. Sex was painful for her and she retreated from him. Not overly sentimental or sensitive, but always practical, Victor explained that he would take care of his sexual needs, which he did in abundance. This did not suit his wife, and she finally divorced him.

Victor accepted life very much as it came, from having a surplus of women with no emotional connection to a wife with physical problems.

Victor recalled when he was just fifteen, he helped a very attractive widow to move. The huge amounts of time he spent with her made the neighbors gossip, and his parents told him he had to stop, but not before he learned a lot about women, in a most pleasing manner.

Once he was asked to father a child to help a wounded veteran who had a lovely wife. He was quite willing and even hoped for an encore, but they disappeared. He heard from a friend that they had a little boy, but it was never confirmed.

Victor had black hair and green eyes, a sort of Victor Mature type. (Victor John Mature was an American stage, film, and television actor who starred most notably in several Biblical movies during the 1950s, and was known for his dark good looks and mega-watt smile).

Victor exuded a certain masculinity. While he was managing the factory, he did his best and was quite successful protecting the women who were often victims of men forcing themselves on the sometimes helpless women. The women were grateful and trusted and liked him. His many affairs with the willing girls from the factory were usually on a little boat he kept, while other girls would act as lookouts to warn him if his then-fiancee Maria was around. Maria was not allowed to spend much unsupervised time with Victor. The family tolerated him sowing his wild oats, hoping that Maria would find a more suitable mate.

Maria was called the Ice Queen, refined and unapproachable. Victor enjoyed the challenge; it stoked his ego that he had won her. Maria's family was at first shocked, but later grew fond of him and were very sad when her young husband was forced to flee.

Years later, he thought his second wife Ethel was basically very decent and civilized in spite of the breakup, so he was not prepared for what he was about to experience. He did remember an instance in Budapest years ago, while he was walking with some friends.

An old gypsy went right up to him, read his palm and told him, "You will cross the ocean far away and marry a whore," then shuffled away not asking for money.

Gypsies were not popular and it was laughed off.

His third romantic relationship happened while he was walking his dog in one of the parks of Griffith Park.

Griffith Park is in Los Angeles, California and has many parks for picnicking and parties; The very famous Griffith Park Observatory where you can visit real stars; the Los Angeles Zoo; Autry Museum of American West a History Museum. ("Gene" Autry was an American singer-songwriter, actor, musician, rodeo performer and business tycoon who gained fame as a singing cowboy in a crooning style on radio, in films and on television for more than three decades beginning in the early 1930's. Autry was the owner of a television station, several radio stations in Southern California, and the LA/CA/Anaheim Angels Major League Baseball team from 1961 to 1997.) Griffith Park also houses Travel town with full size train engines and passenger train cars for everyone to climb up on; pony rides and endless mountain trails to ride horses hike and to be able to see the San Fernando Valley on one side and then the Hollywood Hills on the other side of Southern California, to name only some of the activities plus you are surrounded by Disney Studios, Warner Bros film studio and Universal Studios bordering near-by in the town of Burbank, California.

Victor met a beautiful young girl in the park who went home with him. She stayed a couple of days. The next time he saw her, she had been beaten badly by her pimp for not charging Victor. Victor confronted the pimp, who was very cowardly and took off. Margo explained that she had just started being a prostitute. Victor, after all the things he had seen in his own country, was quite tolerant. She moved in with him, and very soon became pregnant. He brought her to a Catholic hospital, where she had to explain that she was not married. Victor assumed that she was embarrassed, thought that this was his child and his responsibility. He also remembered the gypsy's words and figured, if it's to be, I'll get it over with.

The grim reality of this move began to unfold as Victor discovered that Margo had already given birth to a boy, who had been given away, and a girl that was cared for by Margo's mother and stepfather, despite the fact that the stepfather had been molesting Margo since she was five. It was not surprising that Margo was both a drug addict and an alcoholic, something she concealed for the first few months of marriage.

One night, she threw the baby across the room at Victor screaming, "You love that baby more than you love me!"

Victor should have grabbed the baby and left, but she pleaded that she would change. A fortune was spent on rehab centers. Another pregnancy, this time twin girls.

One day, home from work, Victor found the babies locked in a room, hungry, wet, crying, while Margo was in a local bar. It ended this hellish marriage.

Victor obtained full custody of the three girls and found a home for them with a retired Hungarian school teacher from the Lutheran church. He needed this so that he could earn a living. Victor now had a partner who was a contractor. They built and sold real-estate properties. It was at this time that the Hungarian (Victor) and the Irishman (Keith) were destined to meet.

A realtor told Victor, "You might like him, he has a lot of properties and needs things built. He's not for me, he drives me crazy. He's very charming, but keeps everyone waiting. He's too complicated, I don't have the patience. If you have an appointment with him, be prepared to wait at least an hour."

Victor had been amused by the many tales he heard about this eccentric Irish actor. As many others before him, Victor, after patiently waiting for Keith, decided to drive off, but he made a U-turn when he spotted an elegant Rolls Royce with the top down, piloted, nonchalantly, by a man, who could only be Mr. McConnell. Who else would be shaving with an electric razor while making an illegal left turn, oblivious to the dangers of the road?

The situation that attracted these two was Keith and his perpetually unfinished properties and Victor's skills as a Mr. Fix-it, any problem, any size. They seemed to have an inherent fascination for each other's eccentricities. They understood the complications, unpredictability, and pitfalls through a deep understanding that life doesn't fit a pattern or make sense.

The first time Victor came to Regardless Manor, it seemed more European than any house he had been to in America, so he felt a feeling of comfort, being among friends. The friendship between Keith and Victor grew.

Victor, having put on weight, had a bad haircut, wore polyester uglies, and seemed out of place; however his wit, charm, warmth, and storytelling with his Hungarian accent more than made up for his lacks. He immediately seemed to like me, and as I got to know him, I was impressed by his ability with financing, government requirements, handling labor problems, etc.

I was aware that Victor's feeling for me went beyond friendship. I was used to that and just ignored it. The growing bond between Victor and Keith was genuine. Victor told Keith he was diabetic. He injected himself with insulin daily. Keith immediately took him to a doctor friend, who told him that he could control it with pills. Keith also told Victor that if he died that he would take care of his three children, again without consulting me.

Keith had the type of personality that would evoke strong emotions, admiration, adoration, attachment, fan-like behavior, or jealousy, disdain, even hate. Victor belonged to the first group.

He told me, "I don't know why, but I want to make him a wealthy man so that he can afford his lifestyle."

Keith sustained enormous damage to his properties from earthquake tremors, landslides, to mention a few disasters to the land and homes. Victor was so astute, understanding and filling out the never-ending paperwork, he was able to obtain a $400,000 loan from the Small Business Administration, which at that time was huge for Keith. Victor told Keith he could use the money to buy land and houses and sell them.

Keith had a hard time letting go of anything. I had also suggested that buying and selling was much better than renting to tenants. Keith thought you could outsmart the system; instead he was attracted to a Ponzi scheme, giving him a 15% return.

Victor told him, "You're probably being paid by your own money."

Victor proved to be right.

Victor went with Keith to Keith's bank, looked the documents over and said, "Take your money out right now, today."

Keith refused and two days later his account had been emptied out. Victor said, "If I had promised him millions, I could have taken off with his money, but I just promised him a decent living."

Then there was the other part of the complex Keith. A close friend of mine told me that Keith had a mistress for the past ten years. I had ceased having affairs a long time ago, as I realized they didn't make you happy and someone always got hurt. A continuous ten-year relationship with another woman meant a secret life, perpetual lies, sneaky disappearances, and of course, money. I thought of my work in Chinatown in Los Angeles and then Beverly Hills, in Southern California. Supposedly Keith was managing musicians on those nights, requiring many out of town trips. Many friends knew and thought I knew, but I did not.

The girl was a stunning black model and an American actress, Deborah McGuire, who halfway into the affair married Richard Pryor because Keith refused to divorce me. (Richard Franklin Lennox Thomas Pryor was an American stand-up comedian, actor, and social critic. Pryor was known for uncompromising examinations of racism and topical contemporary issues, which employed vulgarities and profanity, as well as racial epithets. He reached a broad audience with his trenchant observations and storytelling style, and is widely regarded as one of the greatest and most influential stand-up comedians of all time).

Mrs. Richard Pryor divorced her husband after one year of marriage when in one of his drug-induced episodes, he attempted to kill her with a gun. At that time there was a lot of publicity. Had I ever picked up any tabloid, I would have learned sooner. Of course the ever-gallant Keith helped Deborah get her divorce.

Finally, I asked Victor if he had known and he said, "Yes, but I'm Keith's friend, and as much as I care for you, I didn't want you to like me for this reason."

Although the three of us had been close friends for six years, Victor had never made a move towards me, which had always made me feel safe. Because Keith was often absent, Victor and I, his children and mine, went out for meals, movies, and to the beach. When I thought about Keith's flagrant infidelity, I turned to Victor, thinking, he at least seems to really care. I knew this might ruin our wonderful friendship. I was tired of the peacock, I needed the bear, so I thought, the hell with it.

Then the unexpected happened; it was so romantic. If Keith was sexual, Victor was sensual, which was truly rare in men. Victor suited me too well. Maybe for Victor, liking someone, for such a long time with no expectations, made it special for him. We had such feelings for each other; we were happy. Victor was in love, perhaps for the first time in his life. I felt a happiness I couldn't explain. I also realized I hadn't been the perfect wife. Keith's drinking had made me resistant to him. In a way I was happy he had found someone that satisfied him. One can always blame the other person without realizing one's own inadequacies.

As to the continuing relationship with Victor, I told him, "When Keith asks, I will tell him, not before."

It took Keith about a year.

When confronted, I said, "I'm happy with Victor as you seem to be with Debbie. I don't want the boys to be affected."

I realized that I had stopped idolizing Keith, that when one idolizes someone or something, it's because of one's own inner lack. I felt a tremendous sense of relief.

This confession completely unraveled Keith, all the self-control and double standard collapsed.

"What about the family?" He pledged reform.

Victor, not wanting to interfere, asked me to meet him secretly.

I told Victor, "Come over as usual to pick me up. I'm too old to be sneaking out now."

When the two men confronted each other on the staircase, one coming up, the other going down, embarrassment and discomfort was too mild a description. They smiled awkwardly and wordlessly.

I took Keith aside and said, "When you end your situation, then we'll talk."

When Keith returned, he swore the affair with Deborah was over and that the family was the most important and that we should forgive each other. Reluctantly and with a heavy heart, I told Victor.

Victor told me he loved me more than ever because of my decision.

I asked him, "You're not angry?"

He said, "How could I be angry with you? You've given me so much happiness."

He also told me that I could count on him for anything. He gave me access to his bank accounts, perhaps knowing I would never use it. I was deeply touched and really felt loved. At this point, Victor stepped out of the picture.

In pursing one of Keith's exotic business ventures, Keith and I went off to the jungles of Brazil to inspect an opal mine, in which Keith had invested a large amount of money with great expectations. As if in a 'B' movie, a local witch doctor laid his hands on Keith's partner.

The witch doctor turned icy cold when I touched him, and he said, "Bad man, bad man."

Surprise, surprise, the partner turned out to be a con artist. But it takes two to tango, the thief and the greedy innocent. George, my older brother, said that my husband was willing to work sixteen hours a day to avoid working eight.

In 1983, Keith started having a series of symptoms, which turned out to be of all things, ALS (amyotrophic lateral sclerosis, is a progressive neurodegenerative disease that affects nerve cells in the brain and the spinal cord. A-myo-trophic comes from the Greek language. "A" means non. "Myo" refers to muscle, and "Trophic" means nourishment – "No muscle nourishment.").

First my brother, Jean Jacques, then Keith. I was frantic. I brought him to UCLA, University of California, Los Angeles, where for a year and a half they treated him at their world famous medical center, not knowing what he had. Then Robert Brown, a television actor who was most active in the 1960s and 1970s and who was Carroll O'Conner's cousin, told me that Keith's symptoms sounded like David Niven's symptoms, (James David Graham Niven was an English actor, memoirist and novelist. His many roles included Squadron Leader Peter Carter in *A Matter of Life and Death*, Phileas Fogg in *Around the World in 80 Days*, and Sir Charles Lytton in *The Pink Panther*), who also died of ALS. I told the doctors at UCLA, who actually laughed at me, then told me to go to USC, University of Southern California, a privately run University and hospital where they specialized in ALS. I immediately took him.

I asked the doctor in charge, "Why does ALS affect the brain?"

"No, no, it does not," he replied sternly.

"Doctor, I have been to many ALS meetings, and several family members complain of the same thing."

Complete silence.

"Doctor why don't you simply say you don't know?"

He replied smugly, "I'm appearing on PBS (Public Broadcasting Service on television), be sure to watch me," and he gave me the time and date.

As a matter of interest, my brother's symptoms started in his legs, whereas Keith's started in his eyes. Some start in the stomach. David Niven's started with the eyes. I took Keith to a holistic doctor and psychic healers, hoping for a miracle. During this period of deterioration, Keith had bought a Lear jet, sold to him by a drug dealer. He had also invested in an Anaheim brewery, which was located in Anaheim, California near Disneyland. All these financial decisions based on borrowing on the properties including our own home brought us to foreclosure.

By now, Keith had a hard time talking to a pitiful degree. I had counted on my husband's ability to wheel and deal and found myself in a state of confusion and inability to cope with the bombardment of creditors, threats - some terrifying - and legal documents with deadlines I could not meet. I did not call Victor as I felt I had no right to conflict my burdens on him. I put an ad in the Wall Street Journal. All it did was attract sharks that smelled blood. Finally it was Keith with very little voice left who called Victor. The response was immediate as he began to unravel the impossible. Soon we found ourselves at bankruptcy court. To add to the drama, the FBI (Federal Bureau of Investigation) became involved because the jet— now in Keith's name— had been used to transport drugs. The real-estate loans were difficult to renegotiate, based on exaggerated assessments, and so on and so on... A nightmare with no end in sight.

Victor was looking for a new apartment. I proposed that he move into the attic apartment. Keith needed help, and Victor showed me how to give Keith injections, and to make him happy, brought Keith to play golf, all the while valiantly fighting the dreary legal battles. Victor kept the house out of foreclosure by making the payments, which were steep. He knew how much I loved my home.

It was an odd arrangement, but an incredible one, this triangle. It had been three years since Keith and Victor worked together. I had kept my word and had not seen him. I found out Keith had continued to see Deborah, changing only the schedule. I no longer felt that I had to be faithful to my husband, but was discrete. Deborah was scared by Keith's illness and was convinced I was trying to pass him off to her.

I said, "I just wanted you to visit him, because he cares for you. He is my husband and will be with me until he dies."

Life leaves no one out. Richard Pryor developed Multiple Sclerosis and Deborah was with him when he died. The average duration of ALS is about four years, and Keith fit the pattern. He passed away in 1987.

World-renowned physicist Steven Hawking is an exception, with the brain fully functioning. I thought Keith might be an exception, but it was not to be. Carroll O'Connor arranged for Cardinal Mahoney to preside at the funeral, the church was overflowing with friends.

Carroll said to me, "I hope to have as many real friends when I go." Keith was laid to rest at Forrest Lawn.

That was a nice way to end the chapter, but life doesn't end like a movie.

Larry Tierney, (Lawrence James Tierney was an American actor known for his many screen portrayals of mobsters and tough guys, roles that mirrored his own frequent brushes with the law) came up to Victor and me, wagging his finger, yelling, "How could you two do this to Keith?"

Keith had obviously complained to him.

"Did Keith tell you about his girlfriend of ten years?" I asked. "I loved him anyway."

"Oh my God, never mind," muttering while walking away.

How we all judge each other with such righteousness! The fact that I had righteously explained my side to Larry made me feel as if I let Keith down, that I had ruined a wonderful friendship. I felt sad.

Diane and Victor

Chapter 16

To Be or Not To Be

Keith was six foot two, blonde, blue-eyed, refined, elegant, glamorous, and with a wonderful sense of humor. Victor was five foot ten, stocky, dark haired, hooded green eyes, looking very much like a battle-worn Samurai warrior, and badly dressed. What they shared in common was their sense of humor, quick wit, and an "I'll-protect-you-from-the-world" quality that I craved. From Victor I felt he really liked me, as well as loved me. I had always been comfortable with older men. Victor was only four years older, but at one point it doesn't matter, as maturity, finally, hopefully, sets in.

Victor looked older than his years. As I reflected, you live with a person's soul, not their body. Victor wanted to take me to Budapest to meet his family and friends. He told me the only way he could protect me is if he were my husband, as we were going into a communist country. He never proposed, he assumed I would marry him. It kind of amused me as I was not anxious to remarry, but thought the argument made sense. Also, I thought, I'm happy with this man, what more can I expect from this life? And so we were married at the Ritz Carlton Hotel located in Dana Point. Dana Point is a city in Orange County of Southern California. Dana Point Harbor, with its marinas and eclectic unusual strange boutiques, is a jumping off point for dolphin and whale-watching cruises.

Then we were off to Hungary.

The journey was repeated over a dozen times to finalize an ecological project, to clean up the Danube. The Danube Delta is the second largest river delta in Europe, after the Volga Delta, and is the best preserved on the continent, located in Tulcea County, Romania, which the communists had ruined.

By now the communists were gone, Hungary was free. The International Monetary Fund (IMF) had committed a sizable amount of money towards the project. I didn't speak one word of Hungarian, which is not a member of the Indo-European family of languages, but belongs to the Mgyer Altaic, which is shared by Central Asian languages, spoken by Attila the Hun, he was the ruler of the Huns from 434 until his death in March 453. Nevertheless, it was my favorite way to travel, to have a project and be well received by interesting people. I realized why politicians cling onto their positions so desperately as this kind of reception is so much more interesting than the average. I was hoping some would speak French, but only one who was a friend did.

Victor's enthusiasm seemed to make up for his hardships. The people were always charming, especially when they were taking-you-to- the-cleaners, while listening to gypsy music and enjoying wonderful food.

Parallel to working on the public project, Victor was partners in private construction deals.

As the months, then years, then a decade dragged on, I, who had experienced so many confidence schemes with Keith, came to have qualms about the Danube project and the private ones. How can one manage a serious undertaking from a distance? The people on the spot have all the advantages. Victor loved this country and when it transitioned from communist insanity to what seemed to be a glorious future, he was blind to the reality of dishonest things of which he had no knowledge or control. The funding from the IMF seemed to disappear.

Meanwhile back at home in California, he and his partner, Leonard, had been defrauded of valuable properties. Highly respectable attorneys told them it was not a question of winning the case in court, but in addition they would benefit greatly from significant punitive damages. The corruption and the bribery of their adversaries lost Victor and Leonard their case. Leonard succumbed to a massive stroke, no doubt from the stress of seeing a large part of his life's work vanish.

To understand the strength and the recklessness of these two partners, one has to know a little about Leonard. After his discharge from the U.S. Air Force, he opened a bar which was quite successful in New Jersey. He was Jewish, and some people offered to buy his business to force him out. He refused, and his bar was blown up, believing that he and his wife were in there, but fortunately, that night they weren't there. He went directly to the police and told them he knew who did this, but they were of no help. Perhaps they were anti-Semites themselves? Whatever the reason, Leonard, with military experience, waited for an opportunity to resolve this danger to himself and his

family. He waited patiently for the man and his two adult sons to enter their truck and shot all three of them. He shared this information with Victor, but never told his own family, then moved across the country to Los Angeles, in Southern California.

Victor and Leonard became very close. They invested in a gold mine, which needed mining equipment. The mine manager was using chemical leaching compound that was also used to manufacture drugs. The manager was involved in illegal drug preparation sales. Victor and Leonard lost their money, plus it cost them to prove their innocence.

At one time Leonard and Victor were involved in a building project for a prominent charitable organization. The funds came very slowly, so they paid the workers first. When the project ran out of money and they didn't get paid, the project was discontinued. Another one of their ventures was to pick up a plastics factory that had been financed by Lincoln Savings, which was involved in a big scandal. Upon arrival to take over, they found the facility padlocked - they had missed the takeover by one day. One would hope for a reversal of fortune, but it was not to be.

An acquaintance of Victor's asked him to assist in picking up a new Mercedes. The man handed him the keys to open the car door. As Victor walked towards the car, he wondered why the man didn't open it himself. As the man urged him on and he approached the car, two men pushed him onto the hood, handcuffing him and telling him he was under arrest, claiming he was part of a ring of car thieves. Victor's companion had made a deal with the authorities to hand over one of the thieves to reduce his sentence. Victor was sentenced to several months in jail, but was allowed work furlough so that he could support his children. After six weeks, further evidence exonerated Victor and he was released. The judge told him to choose his friends more carefully.

He did have a bit of luck. Keith and I had a friend named Mabel, who lived not too far from us in Laurel Canyon, a very windy road that takes you from the San Fernando Valley over the Santa Monica mountains into Los Angeles near the Beverly Hills area, which is located in the San Fernando Valley, just east of Griffith Park and Los Angeles, California, which was very convenient.

Mabel rented a room to Victor. Mabel had many tenants who did not pay, but Victor paid her without fail. Mabel had always wanted a pool, it seems everyone who lives in the semi desert climate of the San Fernando Valley has a pool, but could not afford it. Even if she could have afforded it, no one would touch it because of the enormous problems with her backyard. At the time, the city was engaged in some improvements just above her house. Victor with his uncanny abilities concocted a deal with the city and they built her a marvelous pool at their expense. Now Mabel decided she wanted more, she wanted him!

He bolted his door from the inside, and when she persisted, he told her bluntly, "You're not my type."

She asked him to leave.

I asked Victor, "Couldn't you have been a little more diplomatic?" But he replied, "No!"

Some of Victor's more amusing adventures happened when he was driving on a day when he was particularly stressed out and was rudely cut off by a small sports car. He followed the driver for several miles, when the sports car finally pulled over. An angry Victor strutted over to the car, and banged on the window.

An athletic man of six foot six came out of the car, towering over Victor and said gently, "Sir, why are you so angry?"

The man turned out to be John "Fred" (Frederick) Dreyer of football fame, and a TV star. Fred is an American actor, star of the hit show *Hunter,* radio host with NBC for seven seasons and currently on CRN iHeartRadio, former American football defensive end for the New York Giants from 1969 to 1971 and the Los Angeles Rams of the NFL (National Football League) from 1972 to 1981.

Victor was disarmed by the gentle response and said, "You're right, I'm going crazy," and the two went out to have a drink.

Another time, on a twisting road, Victor violated a traffic rule and was spotted by a police car; he knew he was being pursued. He was familiar with every nook and cranny of this road, and when he felt he was safe, he victoriously entered Ralph's supermarket lot, but he was immediately deflated, then burst out laughing.

The smiling officer said, "They all come here, all I have to do is wait," and handed him the ticket.

On a personal level, life with Victor was sweet and gentle. I took him to a good barber, he was surprised how much better he looked.

`He asked me about his clothes, "What should I keep?"

I said, "Nothing."

In Hungary, the factory he managed was a textile business and he knew about fabrics, but coming to America he had lost interest in clothing, which was easily remedied. As they say, he cleaned up well. His eating habits had been pretty bad and that was easy to fix, but the years of stress, his bad health habits, and diabetes finally got to him. He had a heart attack in 1994 and had a triple bypass, but he was never the same.

The worst part was the beginnings of the dreaded Alzheimer's disease, a progressive disease that destroys memory and other important mental functions, especially for a man with such a sharp mind. It was devastating to me and I couldn't believe this was happening.

In our apartment, I found a bag with $50,000 in hundred dollar bills, which Victor had systematically been taking out of our account. He was going to send this money to Budapest for more investments. He had asked me if we could invest in more ventures in Hungary.

I said, "NO."

Slowly I began to understand that not all of Victor's brain was functioning.

Victor replied, "I'm glad I asked you."

That's probably when he decided to do it secretly. As things got worse, I had to take Victor's car keys. This was really terrifying to such a macho man, although he took it better than Keith. Another unfortunate issue was that I didn't drive freeways, couldn't drive at night, and had no sense of direction. My son told me I was born without a compass.

Over the years I had questioned Victor about the Danube Delta River project. Why had the IMF funding disappeared? Victor explained he had another source for funding, I said I'd like to meet the people. He was very evasive, this was not the man I knew.

One day I picked up the phone, recognizing a name Victor mentioned regarding the Danube Delta project and started asking questions. The man was very pleasant and said everything was going to be all right, because the Green Lizard People were going to come out of hiding and make themselves known. Oh God, when did this happen?

I was fortunate that I had Kevin, my eldest son, and Susanne, his wife, for moral support. I had already taken Victor's name off the bank accounts so that he could do no more damage.

He had been my hero, saving my home from bankruptcy, and when I sold it, he and Leonard had put the money in their account, which they lost when they lost their case. Nevertheless I was grateful for all his efforts and felt sad that I had to make him so dependent on me, that he had survived such a gruesome operation at that time, when they had to cut his chest open for the triple bypass heart surgery. They have less invasive operations now. I was told that it had probably affected his brain.

Kevin at that time was restoring British sports cars for Hugh O'Connor (Hugh Edward Ralph O'Connor was an American actor and the son of actor Carroll O'Connor known for his role as James Flynn in the 1984 film, *Brass,* and his portrayal as Lonnie Jamison on *In the Heat of the Night* until his death in 1995),who was a very close friend. Carroll O'Connor, who was Hugh's father, was going to open a classic car restoration shop in Newbury Park, California, which is northwest of Los Angeles and in Ventura County. Kevin would be part of the operation, as he is very gifted in automobile restoration.

Unfortunately, Hugh had a very serious drug addiction and ultimately killed himself. Carroll had no real interest after the death of his son, and the business failed. Kevin went back to work for his former employer in the San Fernando Valley, which is in Los Angeles city area and decided he would make more money as a Mercedes automobile technician.

He went to a Mercedes school out of state, passed his exams and came back and worked for a Mercedes dealership. Management policy at the dealership was less than honest, and Kevin would not participate in their practices. As a result, he made less than other men who were exaggerating their bills.

Keith's brother, Paul McConnell, left Kevin with a very rare collector's item - an Irish silver tea set, one of four were made in the world. Kevin and Susanne sold it, and were able to make a down payment on a house. From 2000-2004, the property value doubled.

They sold the house they just bought and Kevin, Susanne, and I combined our resources and bought a five thousand square foot house in a new development in Moorpark in Ventura County, north of Los Angeles, where the eight of us, including four grandsons, were able to live very comfortably.

Victor and I had the very large master suite with double closets, separate toilets, enormous shower and bathtub with jets, a fireplace, built-in refrigerator and sink in the room and a lovely balcony, overlooking the twenty-seven hole golf course. I had beautiful antique furniture, which I brought from my house. Susanne also had beautiful furniture, and with her special artistic talents, created a house that looked remarkably like a 1930's movie set, with its entrance hall and its double winding staircases; a mini mansion.

I was hoping Victor would be pleased, but he was not because he felt he had not provided this for me. Victor died just eight months later in December of 2004. Life is never the way one imagines. I had another house I loved, but no love to share it with. The saddest thing about losing a husband whose mind goes is the feeling of loss and loneliness of a person you shared so much with and is still there, but out of reach, and this was the second time. However, my instincts told me that they are out there somewhere.

Chapter 17

The Supernatural

The following are added additional supernatural events that happened. The interesting thing is that even when I had these experiences, I tended not to take them seriously, but I do want to explain the events that happened and what happen to me.

The earliest one had to do with my mother, who although a fierce atheist, would never have thirteen people at one table. On our way to Barcelona, my Mother met a gypsy she had never seen before. My mother was alone. The gypsy told her that she had three children, two boys and a girl. The eldest boy was extremely intelligent, the younger was gifted in doing business, and the daughter would break many hearts.

George, my older brother, entered the very prestigious University of Southern California (USC) at the tender age of fifteen. Jean Jacques, who temporarily took over my father's business in Hollywood, made a great deal of money in a very short time. Ever since I can remember, I had declarations of love from boys and men. When I was fifteen, a friend of George's took me to a popular hamburger place on the Sunset Strip. The Sunset Strip is the mile-and-a-half stretch of Sunset Boulevard that passes through West Hollywood, California. The restaurant was called "Strips," where they made outstanding hamburgers. There was this man there, who was ten years my senior, and he declared his love for me.

I had finished my hamburger, looked at him, as he had tears rolling down his cheeks, asked very gently, "If you're not going to eat your hamburger, can I have it?"

I wasn't cruel or unfeeling (so I thought), I just figured this was my destiny.

My brothers told me this one. George and Jean Jacques were in Paris together when they bumped into an old Czech friend they knew from Hollywood, California.

After the usual small talk, this friend looked at Jean Jacques and said, "I'm very sorry to tell you this, but you're going to die of a devastating disease."

Jean Jacques died of ALS at the age of forty-three.

The first ghost story I had impressed me. Often people knocked on our door at Regardless Manor to see if we wanted to sell our house. Apparently our house was back in style.

One day a family of five asked if they could visit us as their father, Charles Dorian, an assistant director, had the house built in replica of a mansion he had seen in Bel Air, California, reducing its size. This is where they had been brought up. (Charles Dorian was an American assistant director and film actor He appeared in 26 films between 1915 and 1920. He won an Academy Award in 1933 for Best Assistant Director, and died October 21, 1942 in Albuquerque, New Mexico).

"Of course, please come in."

After chatting with these agreeable people, Kevin, who was twelve at the time, said, "Could I ask you a question?"

He explained that in this very room, he had seen an apparition several times floating in the air, all blue, that looked very much like a woman, and he could see right through her.

They looked at each other and laughed.

"Oh yes, that's Rose and she always dressed in blue head to toe. She died in this room."

Later I asked Kevin why he had never mentioned this to me, he replied, "You never asked."

One evening in the bedroom with the door open, I heard the usual sound of the heavy wooden front door open. It had a distinct sound. Then footsteps on the tile floor in the entrance hall.

"I'm coming," I said.

I went downstairs. There was no one. I was really puzzled, then forgot about the incident.

The following day I was sitting with a girlfriend in the bedroom. We were watching TV. The exact same thing happened. We both went downstairs, again, no one. I explained this odd coincidence to my friend and she ran out of the house screaming. I was happy that at least I had a witness (I wasn't crazy)! For some reason I have never been scared of ghosts, I found it interesting.

I was having friends over for dinner and was cutting food on a large wooden cutting table in the middle of the kitchen, surrounded by all my invited guests. I was facing the opening to the hallway when I heard footsteps, looked up, and saw a blue ball of approximately 4 feet in diameter with a light around it. It was so real to me, I ran after it. My friends were laughing as no one else saw or heard anything. Later, I was told it was a child ghost.

The housekeepers, Norma and Letty, told me over the years, they had seen and heard all sorts of things. I just dismissed them as superstitious Mexican maids. As I look back now, even with my own experiences, one tends not to take others' stories as important. Ego on the alert!

Maureen Olivier, one of Keith's many agents, came to our house with a lady who had just come back from Egypt. She was an anthropologist as well as numerologist (a strange combination). She looked like someone out of an old 1930's movie with her short, masculine gray hair, pleated skirt, and no nonsense Oxford brown laced shoes. She explained that she would like to invest in real-estate with us, and Maureen had given us thumbs up.

When she entered the house, she looked at me intensely for a minute or two, and then said, "Do you realize that you've been mummified in a previous life?"

I looked back at her and said, "Is that why I often sleep with hands crossed over my chest?"

Keith started laughing, and as much as I loved to amuse him, I was telling the truth.

She made no response.

As we were talking, she asked if 8293 was the number of our house.

"Yes," I answered.

"Oh my God, that's a number 4! I can't do business with you, because despite all your efforts, you will lose everything."

Then she left abruptly.

I was superstitious enough to go to the city and have the numbers changed, but to no avail, we still eventually lost everything.

On a lighter note, I was early for work, and I was having a cup of coffee in the Beverly Hilton coffee shop, located at 9876 Wilshire Boulevard, Beverly Hills, California 90210. A woman sitting next to me was telling people's fortunes, just to amuse herself, not charging money.

For fun, I asked, "Can you tell me something?"

"Sure." She looked at me, then said, "Why are there so many flowers in your bedroom?"

I had just redone my bedroom – a floral headboard, floral bedspread, pull-down shades – all floral. My bedroom looked like a garden. It's almost impossible not to believe that there are people with psychic abilities.

One sunny afternoon Keith and I took our children to a party at a park, given by Satya, a Hindu friend from my brother's college days.

He looked at Keith's palm – "You have two wives" – then looked at me and said, "You're very stubborn."

I decided at that time that he was being silly. He would not explain further. He had a crush on me years ago, so I just ignored the whole thing. He was right about my stubbornness, not to mention he was actually right about Keith.

To add to this, one Sunday Keith and I were with friends who brought us with them to see a psychic, who was giving readings in a vacant lot off the Sunset Strip in West Hollywood, California. He had set up a table. There was a fairly large group of people waiting who said this psychic was phenomenal. After quite a wait, Keith sat in front of the psychic. Kevin was standing behind his father. The psychic told Keith that he was deceiving and being very manipulative to someone very close to him.

Kevin told me later that his father told him, "Don't mention this to your mother."

I decided I would try it and was told, "You are being seriously lied to by someone you care for."

My reaction was, "So Keith has affairs. I've always known that. Is it really that important?"

And as usual, I dismissed it.

This incident was basically sad. I ran into my childhood friend Francoise, whom I hadn't seen for a long time. She told me she had become a psychic. My immediate reaction was one of disbelief, as usual.

"I'm so sorry Keith died."

"What are you saying, he's not even sick."

"I was sitting a couple of rows back from you at the Director's Guild, (located at 7920 Sunset Blvd., Los Angeles, California 90046, near Hollywood, California) some time ago and saw black images coming from Keith's head. You only see those when someone is going to die. I saw them so distinctly. I didn't talk to you because I could not bear to tell you."

I had always felt Francoise was not very stable; she had a very difficult childhood.

I replied smugly, "Well, thank God you're wrong."

Not long after, Keith got ALS symptoms. The timing may have been off, but not the prediction. However, nothing is perfect. My next interaction was not with psychics, but rather con-artists. I was feeling desperate when a friend recommended two Frenchmen who came to the house and placed Keith, lying face-up, on our dining table, ran their hands over him, and spoke in an unknown language. After ten minutes, they said he was cured. They asked for no money, but accepted $200 I gave them, thanking them profusely.

At a party given by an Irish girlfriend, Veronica, was an Irish psychic, rather grumpy, who told me I was moving into a wealthy neighborhood and there would be horses around me. Susanne found the house where we live now. There is a riding path, horses, and prosperous people surrounding us.

Francoise came to my house after Victor died. I asked if she could explain the knocking on my bedroom door from time to time, always when I was in bed, but not asleep. It was not the family. They would not tease me in this manner.

She told me it was Victor; that he had been happy with me, and she added, "He's knocking from the inside of your room. I can see him."

I didn't know what to make of it.

My most moving and incredible experience was when I was still living in Regardless Manor. It had only been five months since Keith died. Victor had gone to early morning golf. I was lying there wide awake when the strongest feeling came over me. I absolutely knew that Keith was coming. I suddenly found myself floating in the air and felt Keith's hands in mine. I couldn't see him, but felt his fingers.

"I know that's you."

I cannot tell you in seconds or minutes how long it lasted, but an indescribable joy infused my whole being. I felt a tremendous feeling of peace.

I explained this later to Francoise and she said, "That was a visitation. It happens often after people die."

I'd never heard of this, but when something like this happens to you, it's impossible to deny. One thing that struck me is that all the predictions came true. Also, I was not questioned, but simply told what was to happen. Once again I do not know why I was given this information, but to say the least, it is thought-provoking.

Chapter 18

The Notorious Landlady

Perhaps this chapter should be called "The Tyranny of Tenants." Every business can claim difficulties. When you deal with tenants, it becomes personal and you become part of their problems. When one stops screaming, one can't help laughing.

For me, it started at seventeen when Keith rented out his first piece of property, a small house on the edge of Beverly Hills and the Highland Gorge between Hollywood and Los Angeles, California. He got it in payment for money he had lent to a dress designer who let Keith have the equity he had in the house.

This was the first deal in real-estate for Elaine Young, who had been married to Gig Young. (Gig Young was an American film, stage, and television actor. Known mainly for second leads and supporting roles. Young won an Academy Award for his performance as a slimy dance-marathon emcee in the 1969 film *They Shoot Horses Don't They?*. He died October 19, 1978 in Manhattan, New York City, New York, from a gunshot wound as a murder-suicide).

Elaine had Warren Beatty as her client. (Henry Warren Beatty is an American actor and filmmaker. He has been nominated for fourteen Academy Awards – four for Best Actor, four for Best Picture, two for Best Picture, two Best Director, three for Original screenplay and one for adapted screenplay). The house was fully furnished and he took it.

After a while Beatty said he was moving. I was anxious to help Keith and asked Beatty if I could move the furniture back into the place as there were prospective tenants coming to look at the house. He had moved all the furniture in one corner of the room and lived that way.

When everything was in order he said, "You know, it looks better that way."

He left owing rent that was never paid, but at least there was no damage. Called his agent - no help - a taste of the future.

If Keith was not good at managing properties, he was excellent at acquiring them and the problems that accompany them. A three - bedroom house in Laurel Canyon was rented by an elegant lady with a little girl and a black maid. A few months later, the house had been trashed. I scrubbed the walls, which were covered with graffiti and other damage. While I was there, two nice looking men from the Vice Squad appeared at the door. Apparently, the lady had been running a brothel for lesbians.

One of the men said, "Why do you rent to those kind of people?"

I replied, "Tell you what. You find the tenants, and I'll only rent to people you approve of."

They smiled and walked away.

After four days of cleaning, Keith said, "I don't want you to work this hard, I'll get some help."

A house in the Hollywood Hills had been rented and abandoned.

I went with the workman to inspect the house, I said, "What is that terrible smell?"

The workman, who had already been there said, "Oh, that's only the leopard."

There was a leopard in a cage that had been left there, not to mention the helpful workman, who was slowly helping himself to items in the house, including all the draperies.

One of the more comical moments with tenants occurred when a youngish, good-looking man rented one of our houses also located in the Hollywood Hills. He told us he published a magazine called *The American Sexual Freedom League*, and did we have any objections?

"Hugh Hefner seems to be prospering. Any problems with your finances?"

He seemed to be financially qualified and moved in. Soon afterward, he invited us to a cocktail party. As usual with Keith, we arrived late. We were greeted by our host attired in a smoking jacket, perhaps mimicking Hugh Hefner. (Hugh Marston Hefner was an American businessman, magazine publisher, and playboy. He was the founder of *Playboy* and editor-in-chief of the magazine, which he founded in 1953.) He led us into the living room, which was filled with what I can only describe as a dense pink fog. It didn't make me cough, but apart from already having poor eyesight, I couldn't see a thing and clutched onto Keith.

I asked the host why the fog, and he replied, "For privacy."

As the pink fog cleared up in pieces, I looked around and saw a hefty, totally nude woman sitting on the couch. We were told that if we wanted to use a room in the back, we were very welcome to do so. I could hear soft murmurings around me and saw dim figures, half clothed. A couple came towards us in their underwear, not particularly attractive, but not threatening, polite, told us about themselves. He worked in a lab, she was a housewife. They lived in the San Fernando Valley north west of Los Angeles and this is how they spiced up their sex lives. They asked if we would like to join them.

'Oh, I'm so sorry, but we were on our way to the airport and just wanted to say hello." I was hoping they didn't feel rejected.

Our host asked if we would like a complimentary copy of the magazine.

"Thank you so much."

As we made our way out of the pink fog into the fresh night air, we both laughed – not with a sense of superiority, but with relief that there were no awkward moments.

Another incident happened with a house we owned at the corner of the street where we lived, where the people thought Keith and I were on a trip. They were fleeing and taking the furniture, they left the door open as they hadn't finished stealing.

Keith said to me, "Don't go in, it's against the law."

"Oh really? Watch me." No one was in, but I left a note - Bring everything back and leave!" They did.

Then there was the house we had built near Lake Hollywood across from Merv Griffin's house. (Mervyn Edward Griffin Jr. was an American television host and media mogul. He began his career as a radio and big band singer who went on to appear in film and on Broadway in New York. From 1965 to 1986, Griffin hosted his own talk show, *The Merv Griffin Show).*

Three contractors, the last one moved in and had to be removed. After nearly five years, it was rented to a man, Mister Brown, who on the first night, burnt half the house down.

Two years later, a Mister Brown called, "Remember me? I'm the one that accidentally burned your house. I really liked that house. Could I re-rent it?"

It seemed we had particularly strange times when the houses were newly built. We had two houses built on Lime Orchard Road in Beverly Hills, California, off of and near Coldwater Canyon, which ran from the San Fernando Valley up the windy hills and into Beverly Hills on the other side, which also took forever because Keith was all charm and had no knowledge of who to hire. They were right below Charlton Heston's property. Charlton Heston was an American actor an political activist. As a Hollywood star, he appeared in almost 100 films over the course of 60 years. He died April 5, 2008 in Beverly Hills, California.

One particular man, a Colonel Baumgarden, came in a wheelchair accompanied by a caretaker. He paid his rent in cash, first and last month. The Colonel, who was inside the house at the door, handed the money to Keith and said, "And that's the last money you'll ever see from me," and slammed the door in Keith's face.

Later it was discovered he was a fink for the FBI and was very protected. When he left, he also left two live raccoons in the furnished house. Enough said, also a lot of unpaid rent.

One story was a little more whimsical and happened when I was on one of my trips to Tahiti. I was sitting at an outdoor cafe, listening to three young Americans struggling with the waitress to make themselves understood.

I said, "Let me help you," and spoke to the waitress in French to explain their order.

They started talking and said they had just come from Los Angeles, California where they had rented a home for a short time in Laurel Canyon and were charmed by the delightful Irish owner, Keith. They left with no money owing - small world.

Good stuff doesn't last long. There were extremely heavy rainfalls one year and Charlton Heston's back garden, which was situated above one of our houses, fell down heavily damaging our property. Keith did not handle the situation well, and Victor was not around at the time.

We had built a house with a pool on the vacant lot next door to our own home. It was rented to what seemed to be pleasant enough people, they had a Mercedes in the garage. All of a sudden the rent stopped coming with nothing but promises.

After three months of no payments and a large party around the pool, given by the tenants, I went over and announced, "Do you realize your charming hosts haven't paid their rent in three months?"

They all disappeared inside. A couple of days went by, no sign of anyone, the house was locked, the door wasn't answered, and the car was not in the garage (it had been repossessed as we later found out). I broke a window to get in. They were inside and immediately called the police. The police came and they told me I couldn't do that. I explained that I thought the house was abandoned.

One policeman took me aside and said, "If you ever need to shoot someone, make sure you drag them inside."

After Sal Mineo was murdered in 1976, his house was for sale in the Hollywood Hills and we bought it. (Salvatore Mineo, Jr., was an American film and theater actor, known for his performance as John "Plato" Crawford opposite James Dean in the film *Rebel Without a Cause)*. We went to see the damage. He had fourteen cats living there.

Keith said, "Oh my God, I can't stand the smell."

I was always trying to save Keith money and said I would clean it, but it had to be redone. It was soon rented to a screenwriter and his wife who became close friends with us. The house was treated decently, so that was a reprieve of the disasters awaiting.

Maman, after Papa's death, stayed in Hawaii, and bought houses one by one, redid some, then resold them always at a profit; she definitely had an eye for it. She came to visit me and the family and an old friend of hers, Georgette, a native of New Caledonia, which is a French territory comprising dozens of islands in the South Pacific. Georgette who started out selling Avon cosmetics door to door, then invested in a chinchilla farm and finally ended in real-estate in Hollywood, making a fortune. Good old USA - from makeup to millions!

Georgette showed Maman the famous Spanish Moorish building "Patio Del Moro." It had been built in 1925 by Arthur and Nina Zwiebell, the architectural designers. The Zwiebells were famous for their innovation in the design of courtyard apartments in Southern California. Since they were not architects, they hired Leland Bryant, one of the most renowned architects of the era to implement their designs. His legacy includes The Sunset Towers, The Mirador, Savoy Plaza, Colonial House, Harper House, La Fontaine – the list is endless of the remarkably talented man.

"Patio Del Moro" was influenced by Cairo, Beirut, Baghdad, and Madagascar, which was very *a la mode* in those days, very much due to Hollywood films. Courtyards with fountains, floral murals, Moorish entrances, and elaborate patterned hand-painted tiles, and a turret on top.

Located on Fountain Avenue in West Hollywood, California, "Patio Del Moro" had been extremely popular, housing Charlie Chaplin (he was an English comic actor, filmmaker and composer who rose to fame in the era of silent film, know for his character "The Tramp"), Paulette Goddard (was an American actress, a child fashion model and a performer in several Broadway productions as a Ziegfeld Girl; she became a major star of Paramount Pictures in the 1940s), Buddy Rogers (was an American professional wrestler), Joan Fontaine (was a British-American actress best known for her staring roles in Hollywood films; she appeared in more than 45 feature films in a career that spanned five decades), Troy Donahue (was an American film and television actor and singer, popular sex symbol in the 1950s and 1960s), Susanne Pleshette (was an American actress and voice actress, she started in the theater and began appearing in films in the late 1950s such as *Rome Adventure* and Alfred Hitchcock's *The Birds*), "Johnny" Mark Galecki (an American actor, known playing Leonard Hofstadter in the CBS sitcom *The Big Bang Theory* since 2007 and David Healy in the ABC sitcom *Roseanne* from 1992 to 1997), and many more. Maman had found a treasure.

When Maman bought it in 1963, it was fully rented, but by whom!? Maman hired a management company and returned to Hawaii. Big mistake! Unless you have a trusted staff of people that work for you, it is next to impossible to be far away from your business. Maman had dealt with all of her houses directly in Hawaii. Talk about from the frying pan into the fire.

The tenants became worse, repair bills multiplied; revenues shrank with the incompetence and the thievery of the management company. One tenant had eighteen leaks and showed the eighteen buckets she used when it rained, but she wouldn't move, she loved the apartment. I was now married to Victor, who knew construction, and I convinced my mother to let Victor and me manage the building. Victor explained that she should refinance the building to have smaller payments. She'd have a bigger income and have money for the essential repairs that had to be done.

There was a doctor in the largest apartment, who had not paid in three years. This is a rather strange story, but quite true. I had a friend who claimed to be a "white witch." The doctor had used every legal means to avoid paying his rent, so my friend "the witch" and I went to a mystic store, where she purchased oil that was to ensure the person in question would leave within three days if the oil was rubbed on the front doorknob. Believe it or not, the doctor was gone three days later. One could speculate that he had used up all his ways of delaying the departure. Hocus Pocus? Thank God! Maman couldn't believe it.

In February of 1995, Maman died at the age of eighty-six. The funeral was held at the Outrigger Club where she had been a member for many years. George and I were to go on a canoe and toss the ashes in the ocean, but all of a sudden there was a downpour and all the guests were brought to Maman's house, which was very close by. The Outrigger club was supposed to call when it stopped raining; two hours passed, no call. George called and was told, "Oh, some of the boys took out the ashes in a canoe for you."

It was ironical, because Maman had always said she didn't believe in funerals. The Outrigger Club apologized and said to bring friends for lunch the following day, when George and I could take the canoe and throw leis on the water, which we did.

Back to "Patio Del Moro" where the problems were mounting. There was an actress who paid faithfully, but stole things out of people's apartments, and when she was drunk, she would go out in the courtyard totally nude. One day, one of the nicer tenants complained of having his mail stolen. The actress happened to have her car parked in front of "Patio Del Moro". The tenant, through the window of her car, saw a package on the front seat addressed to him that he had been expecting. When confronted, she gave it back.

I asked the tenant to go to the police with me, but the answer was, "No I don't want to get involved."

A typical answer from many tenants. It seems to be a very human response to problems. I tried to get her evicted twice, but failed as no one wanted to get involved. I decided to calm myself down and not be so angry, and even be polite. One day after having a chat with her, the actress asked me if I knew a good manager for a twenty-seven unit building she owned in the San Fernando Valley.

I went to the building and found the manager, who turned out to be the woman's brother. "Oh my God, my sister is a kleptomaniac and a pathological liar. Why are you letting her live there?" he said.

I thought *I'll take care of this when the opportunity arises.*

Meanwhile, another tenant called from Las Vegas and said he wouldn't be able to pay the rent for a while.

"And what shall I tell the bank?" I asked. "Sorry I don't have any money? I'm sorry but you'll have to leave."

"How can you treat me this way after I've told you the truth?"

The tenant decided to sabotage the water pipes, which was rather costly.

Then there was the wealthy young girl who rented the apartment, took off to India with a Guru, and came back with a little baby. She had the front door of her apartment weathered and beaten so that it looked like the poorest part of India, all without permission. Then one day, she had a large rickety iron bed, completely rusted, which she had brought from India. I told her that it would not fit in the front door and if she wanted it, it would have to be taken apart. Fortunately for all, it fell apart. The topper was when she called and said there was a leak. I had, had the wooden floors finished recently and rushed over to find the girl with baby in arms, standing in front of a waterfall in the apartment.

"Couldn't you have called me sooner?"

This had been going on for days. Her father was a wealthy property owner who did not want his own daughter as a tenant.

In December of 1995, Victor had a triple bypass, cardiac surgery. I, in a frantic state, was told by a couple who had been in the building for quite some time, articulate and pleasant, they suggested that they would oversee and rent out the units for a reduction in their rent. I was extremely grateful as Victor needed a lot of care. At the beginning it seemed to work. I realized that after the operation Victor had changed notably. He recuperated, but his mind was slowly deteriorating.

The apartments were all rented at low prices, that I found out later were not the prices being charged and that the couple was pocketing the difference. I also discovered that the couple was filming porn movies in their apartment with the cast entering and exiting through the rear garage door, down through the cellar and on to their private patio. I decided to stop this by changing the lock on the cellar door. The tenant threatened me with a saw in his hand.

Victor tried to protect me by getting between us, the tenant screaming, "You're ruining my life."

By this time, people gathered around and the man ran off. The legalities I encountered in the situation were unfair and ridiculous.

I realized I was completely in charge and had to make decisions. I saw Kevin overworked and underpaid, because he wouldn't cheat his customers.

I said to Kevin, "Quit your job, we'll share whatever there is."

This was the third triangle in my life. That was the best decision I ever made. Susanne and Kevin were extraordinarily talented and hardworking to the point of exhaustion. The other choice would have been to sell the apartment building at a low price, as there were constant offers. There were rats jumping from banana tree to banana tree, one cellar had five feet of water, there were drug addicts in some apartments.

Susanne looked at the building and remarked, "We'll have to tame this place," and that's exactly what was done.

Kevin took care of the thieving actress, went to court, was able to get witnesses, and had her put out. There was more refinancing as money was needed for the renovations. Even though Victor had taken care of the immediate repairs, this building was not his forte.

"Patio Del Moro" had been in decline for forty odd years. The abuse and neglect had taken its toll. Whatever savings I had plus selling most of my jewelry all went into the building. Kevin, because of his meticulous work as a Mercedes mechanic and restoring antique cars (in one show he won first place), he had knowledge that helped with the plumbing, electrical and roofing problems, along with Susanne's abilities to create, design, recreate existing artwork with museum quality, and together created a building that was more beautiful than when it was first built and it attracted a better group of tenants. Because of the huge restoration, the rent soared. With five years of dedication, struggle and sacrifice, a masterpiece emerged. My secret wish was that I could have just given tours, rather than have tenants.

In our house in Moorpark, the buyer had to be responsible for their own landscaping; Susanne created all the landscaping surrounding the house. The back garden took the longest of all because the monies had been poured into "Patio Del Moro". Susanne created with her marvelous sense of beauty what I like to think of as a garden of reflection.

This garden is where I reflect on my life and realize as I sit, think, and read - "Your ego is an attempt to perceive yourself as you wish to be, not what you are."

I have always been uncomfortable with the phrase "I gotta be me." What I see now is a trembling, indignant ego, wondering why the world doesn't recognize who "me" is! Ego, ego, when will I let you go?

I also realized I don't own another person nor am I owed anything. Most of all, I realized my life is my own perception. I can see now that my laziness, fatigue, insecurities are all based on fear. I have learned that "truth is simple – complexity is of the ego." This makes complete sense to me and as I become more aware, I find more peace.

Voltaire, known by his nom de plume, real name, Francois-Marie Arouet, was a French Enlightenment writer, historian and philosopher famous for his wit his attacks on Christianity as a whole, especially the established Catholic Church and his advocacy of freedom of religion, freedom of speech and separation of church and state said, as I noted before, "It is not more surprising to be born twice than once."

The pure logic of that quote astounded me. I've come to understand that we project our lives and are responsible for our decisions. I have never felt victimized, but realized as one's awareness grows, one suffers less. I would rather laugh at life than cry about it. I tell the truth because I don't see the point in lying. Without a spiritual overview, it's practically impossible to understand anything in this world. What I do know is that I don't know. That's a step in the right direction. I now realize that if "Hollywood" is an illusion, then so is the rest of the world. With these thoughts, I bid you adieu.

Patio Del Moro

www.ingramcontent.com/pod-product-compliance
Lightning Source LLC
Chambersburg PA
CBHW021223090426

42740CB00006B/354